HOMESTEAD ON THE RANGE

A Tenderfoot Girl in Wyoming

PEARL MIRICH

Published by
Diane (Mirich) Barrett

Illustration by
Carol (Mirich) Sokoloff

Cover by
Karri Klawiter

Homestead on the Range
Copyright © 1994 by Pearl (Rumble) Mirich
All rights reserved.

Without limiting the rights under copyright reserved above, no part of this publication may be reproduced, stored in or introduced into a retrieval system, or transmitted, in any form, or by any means (electronic, mechanical, recording, photocopying, or otherwise) without the prior written permission of the copyright owner of this book.

ISBN 978-1-7350520-0-7

for my family

Carol Sokoloff

CONTENTS

1. A Letter from the Homestead
2. The Train Trip
3. The Arrival and the Surprise
4. The Homestead
5. Life on the Homestead
6. Exploring
7. Milk Merchants
8. The Pony Deal
9. Driving in the Ponies
10. Breaking Ponies
11. To the Hills for Wood
12. The Quarry
13. Ruth and Betty
14. The Pack-Saddle Camping Trip
15. Goodbye to Snowball and Midnight
16. Billy Goat
17. Runaway
18. Whang
19. Visit to Frenchy and Marguerite
20. Edna and Ruth
21. The Flood
22. A Barn Dance
23. The Return
24. A Letter Home
25. Haying
26. Letter to Ruth
27. Phebe and Teague
28. An All Day Ride
29. Unexpected Opportunity
30. The Rodeo
31. Farewell

1. A Letter from the Homestead

Iron Mountain, Wyoming
May 25, 1928

Dear Pearl,

School is out now. It's great to be back home with Mother. I don't like to have to work for my room and board in Cheyenne so I can go to school. I'll have to do it three more years though to get my diploma.

I'm glad you'll soon be here. I have a great plan for us to earn some money this summer. It will be a lot of fun too.

You remember that Charlie Farthing, the rancher whose land surrounds our homestead, has hundreds of Shetland ponies. He sells some every year. The ponies are sold untrained. My plan is to make a deal with him. We'll suggest that he let us run in ten or a dozen of them and tame them so children can ride them. He could sell them at a much higher price.

What do you think of my plan? I have plenty of other ideas for a fun summer too.

See you soon.

Love,

Evelyn

P.S. I have a surprise for you when you get here.

Pearl ran to find her own mother. "I want to read Evelyn's letter to you. She has the most wonderful idea for us to earn some money."

Evelyn was Pearl's niece but they were both seventeen years old, Pearl being the elder by only a few months. Evelyn lived on a homestead in Wyoming with her sister, Arlynn, her half-brother, Jackie, and her mother, Marie, who was Pearl's older sister by fifteen years. Pearl, the youngest in her large family, lived with her parents in Cedar Rapids, Iowa.

After hearing the letter Pearl's mother said, "If Marie thinks it is possible for you to train ponies, I guess it's all right. But first we must ask your father about it."

"Mother, I'm sure that Evelyn has permission from Marie or she wouldn't have written about this. You know Evelyn broke her mare, Waltina. And Marie knows how to train horses."

"Your father and I will discuss this tonight after dinner, Pearl."

Pearl was worried about what her father would say. Her mother and father made all important decisions together. They talked things over in private and then announced their joint decision. They avoided saying no; they wanted to give their children as much freedom as possible. However, if their decision was negative, it could not be changed by any amount of importuning.

Pearl's mother was an optimist. She believed that her children could do anything. Pearl's father, in contrast, tended to focus on difficulties and obstacles. Pearl thought that in these private conferences it must be that her mother was usually able to persuade her father to say yes. Otherwise would sister Marie have been able to get their financial backing for her venture in homesteading in Wyoming? Marie was in her early twenties when she undertook this daring step. Breaking ponies was different though. Maybe her father would think it too dangerous.

After dinner Pearl went to the home of one of her friends to study. She stayed only about an hour and a half and then hurried home. Her parents were in the living room reading the paper when she arrived. "Can I do it? Can I help Evelyn break ponies?" she blurted out the minute she entered the house.

"Your mother and I think it will be all right, Pearl. Marie will see that you do everything wisely. Jack often broke horses for neighboring ranchers. Marie knows how he went about it. She's very good with horses too. And Evelyn has had a lot of experiences with horses. But you're a city girl. You must be very careful."

"Thank you, Father! Thank you, Mother! I'll be careful. I really want to do this. I love ponies. It will be so much fun."

"It will be hard work and dangerous too, Pearl. Pay strict attention to everything Marie tells you," her father warned.

"I will, Father."

"You can try this, Pearl. But if it proves to be too difficult or dangerous, you and Evelyn must not continue with it. You can change your mind, you know."

"All right, Father. That's fair enough. We'll try it. I'm sure we can do it though. I'm going to write Evelyn now."

Pearl went to the dining room table, opened her notebook and began writing a letter to her niece. After writing a few sentences she put down her pen and leaned her chin on her hand, dreaming about the Farthing ponies. She had heard the story of these ponies many times. In 1886 the grandfather of rancher Charlie Farthing had imported two Shetland ponies from Scotland for his children. When the children grew up the ponies were turned loose on the range and the family lost track of them. They supposed that they had died. Many years later when Charlie Farthing was riding in the hills he came across a band of Shetlands. Later, other bands, always led by a dominant stallion, were discovered. There were about one thousand ponies. The rancher realized that here was another source of income. He and his two sons, Tom and Merrill, rounded up the ponies, branded them and castrated the males. They bought stallions to bring in new blood. Every year they sold some of the ponies and they had reduced their number to about four hundred.

Pearl wanted to see all four hundred of them, and she imagined how she and Evelyn would choose the most beautiful ones to train.

Finally Pearl stopped daydreaming and finished her letter. She went into the living room and said, "I wonder how many ponies Mr. Farthing will let us train? It will be such fun to have a lot of ponies to ride."

"Remember you'll only have three months," her father warned. "You can't train very many in that short a time."

"Marie can probably tell you how many," Pearl's mother suggested.

Pearl had already spent several summers on her sister's homestead. When she was there, she and Evelyn were constant companions. They almost lived outdoors, riding horseback every day, helping with the chores and roaming about the prairie.

Pearl was the youngest of a family of eight: two boys, Earl and Herbert who were the first and second children, followed by six girls – Marie, Phebe, Edna, Ruth, Elisabeth, and Pearl. Marie was the oldest of the girls. She married very young and had her two daughters. Her marriage was unhappy and finally ended in divorce. For several years Marie and her daughters lived with her parents and Pearl in their large home in the little college town of Mt. Vernon, Iowa. Then after a trip to visit a friend in Wyoming, Marie decided to homestead there. She took seven year old Evelyn to Wyoming with her and left Arlynn, three years old, in Iowa with her parents.

Marie had filed on 640 acres (one square mile) of land in southeastern Wyoming. The original Homestead Act passed in the 1860's permitted a person to file on only 169 acres of government land. By making certain specified improvements and living on the homestead the required number of months out of each of five years, the homesteader could "prove up" his claim and obtain ownership of the property. Because so much land was needed on the dry western plains to pasture animals – up to twenty-five acres for each one – the law was changed. In 1906 the Kincaid Act provided that in certain areas a homesteader could file on four times as much land (640 acres) and prove-up in only three years.

Marie was like a second mother to Pearl. Although Pearl was a homebody, she was never homesick staying with her sister. When Marie came back home to live after divorcing her husband, Pearl was five years old. Evelyn and she went to kindergarten, first and second grades together. Marie made them dresses that were alike. She made perfect divinity and fudge and popcorn balls for all the children. They hung around Marie when she made ice cream, cookies and cake and she let them lick off the dasher from the ice cream freezer and scrape out the frosting bowls.

When May Day came Marie helped them make beautiful May baskets out of pastel-colored tissue paper which they cut into fringed bands and wrapped around boxes. They carried May baskets filled with candy and popcorn, with violets and other spring flowers, to their friends' homes. They hurried to the door, hung the baskets on the doorknob, knocked on the door and then ran away. If they were caught, they would get kissed. They ran as though they thought that was a horrible fate!

On Valentine's Day Marie helped the children make valentines. Pearl and Marie's father was a contractor for painting and wall-papering and he brought home sample wallpaper books with the elaborate patterns favored then – flowers, birds, in every color. The girls had fun choosing the ones they thought were the prettiest for making original valentines. Pearl had beautiful memories of Marie and loved her dearly. She looked forward eagerly to summers with her.

Marie had married again after she had been in Wyoming a few years. Her husband was Jack Achttien, a cowhand, silversmith, and blacksmith. Jack's parents were immigrants from the Netherlands, who had established a dairy farm near Indianapolis, Indiana. They had old-world ways and were struggling to get ahead in their new country. Perhaps they were strict and demanded too much of their two daughters and son. When Jack was sixteen years old he ran away from home, went west and never let his parents know he was alive and well. After he married Marie, she persuaded him to establish contact with them. They were overjoyed. There was another daughter now. The two older sisters were teachers; the youngest one was in grade school. Members of the family visited Jack and Marie every year.

Marie and Jack had a son named after his father. He looked like his father – very blond curly hair and blue eyes. Their marriage was a happy one.

Pearl loved Jack. He was full of fun and generous. He and Marie took her to the famous rodeo, Cheyenne Frontier Days, one summer. He gave Pearl five dollars to spend. Pearl had never had so much spending money. When the rodeo was over she still had most of the money. Jack was an artist in working with silver. He could make beautiful silver mounted bridles. He was a skilled blacksmith too. Pearl liked to watch him shoe the horses and affix metal rims to wagon wheels, make bits and branding irons. He could also ride broncs. Pearl remembered his riding a bucking horse while holding a cigarette in one hand. He was training this horse for some rancher.

He and Marie were worried about Pearl's health. The first time she went to Wyoming she was twelve years old. She wasn't very well. She was very skinny. Jack teased her about this and once named a scrawny calf Pearl. Pearl didn't care because she knew Jack liked her. He and Marie believed that outdoor life in the sunshine and fresh air of Wyoming could make her strong. They were saving money to buy her a railroad ticket to Wyoming the next summer.

Then tragedy struck. In the spring Pearl and several of her siblings were having a happy time in Iowa at a cabin on the Wapsipinicon River when they received a telegram notifying them that Jack had been dragged to death in a horseback accident. He was working on the Inness ranch, rounding up cattle for branding. That day he rode a strange horse. At the end of the day he playfully roped one more animal. A good roping horse will move away from a roped animal, keeping the rope taut at all times. But this horse acted up and allowed the rope to slacken. The rope then entangled one of Jack's feet in the stirrup. The saddle, strained by the pull of the rope, slipped, and the horse ran.

Jack was dragged over the rocky ground. The rancher's elder daughter managed to ride alongside the runaway and grasp the bridle, but it came off in her hand. It was a fancy bridle that fit over just one ear. It didn't have the headstall which fastens to the cheek strap.

Marie was crazy with grief when the news reached her. By mere chance Pearl and Marie's father had just arrived in Wyoming for a visit, so he took charge, made arrangements for a funeral and burial in Cheyenne, and sent word home. Marie and Pearl's sister Ruth was teaching country school in Wyoming and she comforted Marie as best she could.

Because of the necessity to care for her small son and fulfill the responsibilities of the homestead, Marie gradually overcame her worst grief. But she was often melancholy and at these times the girls knew she was thinking of Jack.

2. The Train Trip

Pearl's small trunk was packed and repacked. Her mother kept adding things she wished to send to Marie. Pearl was collecting books to take along. She couldn't live without books. Marie and Evelyn loved to read too. Often Pearl got out the things she had ordered from the Sears catalog and imagined riding across the wide prairies of Wyoming. She unrolled the lariat and thought about how she would become an expert roper even though when she tried using the lariat she couldn't do anything with it. She was proud of the fact that she had earned the money for these purchases and for part of her round-trip ticket by baby-sitting for fifteen cents an hour.

Whenever she heard the haunting whistle of a steam engine, she wished that she were aboard – on her way once more to her sister's homestead. She loved being there. It was such a contrast to city life in Cedar Rapids, where the family moved about a year after Marie settled in the West. There she would enjoy an active outdoor life. Everything would be completely different. She was more than willing to give up the comfort of her home for her sister's little shack. Roughing it in Wyoming was much more attractive than trying to find something interesting to do in the city. The days crept by. The weeks were endless. School dragged on. She daydreamed in class. Her history teacher noticed her faraway look and often called on her to recite when she had no idea what was being discussed. She thought of a strategy to avoid this problem. She studied hard and listened attentively while gazing out the window. When the teacher called on her, she responded with the correct answer. After a few times the teacher stopped concentrating on her.

Finally, the day of release came. School was out. The next day her parents took her to the depot where she and her mother stood in a long line waiting to buy a ticket, while her father waited to check her trunk in the baggage room. The station was thronged with travelers and people seeing them off. There was a hum of many voices, interrupted now and then by the station master calling out in a booming voice the departure of trains and intoning the names of cities through which they would pass. His voice echoed with a hollow sound in the high-ceilinged waiting room, causing a distortion so one could hardly recognize the names: "Omaha, Grand Island..." Pearl was listening for these places that were on her route. They had a long wait because Pearl was so worried about missing the train and so eager to begin her journey that she had insisted they get there early.

"Remember, don't get off the train when it stops for fifteen or twenty minutes at a station," her mother said. "We usually do get off when we travel together, but you will be alone this time and you must stay on the train."

"If anyone annoys you, tell the conductor," her father said. "He'll be coming through the cars often to collect tickets. Here's some money so you can buy dinner tonight in the dining car. You can buy some candy and gum too from the vendors on the train."

Her mother gave her a large paper bag. "Here's some lunch I packed for you, Pearl. There are cheese sandwiches, some fried chicken, apples, oranges, and cookies. You can buy milk on the train."

"Write to us as soon as you arrive," her father admonished.

"Tell Marie I may come out later for a week or so," her mother said. "And give our love to her and the girls."

Pearl assured them that she would do just as they said and thanked her mother for the lunch and her father for the money.

"Remember," Dad reminded her, "you change from the Union Pacific line to the Colorado and Southern in Cheyenne, Pearl. The Dunns will be at the station to see you aboard."

"Then you get off at Altus. Marie will be there to meet you," her mother added.

At last her train arrived. They went out to the platform. Pearl shrank back as always when the huge black noisy engine with its enormous drive wheels passed her. Then there was a rattling stop and the monster blew out threatening jets of steam. She could see the fireman. His job was to shovel coal from the coal car behind him into the glowing fire box to make steam for the boiler. There was a strong smell of coal smoke. She could feel the heat of the engine. She saw the man who oiled the engine begin his work. His oil can had a very long, thin spout.

After the arriving passengers got off, Pearl and her parents entered a coach. Her mother asked a pleasant-looking lady, "May our daughter sit with you? She's traveling to Cheyenne alone."

The lady moved some things from the seat by the window and said, "I'll be glad to have the company and look after her. But I go only as far as Omaha."

"Thank you very much," her father said. "Pearl, you can ask some other nice lady if you can sit with her when you get to Omaha."

All admonitions were repeated. Then her parents kissed Pearl goodbye and got off the train. They stood by the coach window and tried to communicate some last messages through gestures, a futile effort. So they were probably all relieved when the conductor finally called, "All aboard," and the train started. The engine struggled to get the cars moving. As each car started in succession the passengers were jolted. When all the cars had started rolling, the jerky movements stopped and the train slowly picked up speed. The "clickety-clack, clickety-clack" of the wheels worked up to a rapid tempo.

Pearl loved riding on the train. Seated on a stiff bench seat, with red, scratchy upholstery she contentedly began a journey of over eight hundred miles. It grew hot, so the windows had to be opened. Soot from the smokestack blew in and begrimed everything. Sometimes cinders got into her eyes. These discomforts were accepted as part of train travel. It was an adventure to take a train journey.

The conductor came by, taking tickets and tearing off a portion, leaning across the passengers to put the stub in a holder between the windows. Vendors began to peddle their wares. "Sandwiches – cheese and ham!" "Soda pop, candy, gum!" "Apples!" These cries made Pearl think of food and she began munching on an apple. As the journey continued it appeared that train travel made people hungry. At any given time a lot of people were eating. This made others think of food and they would start in. This was one way to pass the time.

Looking out the window at the green countryside and farms was pleasant. Then the constant procession of telephone poles, which seemed to rush by so close to her face, made her dizzy. So she began observing her fellow passengers. People were friendly. There was much visiting back and forth. They helped entertain children and shared papers and magazines.

A good thing about train travel, Pearl thought, is that you can get up and walk around. Just sitting is tiresome and hard on the legs. There was constant movement back and forth from the seats to the toilets, and to the water cooler recessed into a wall at one end of the car. Here passengers could get a cold drink from flimsy paper cups. The smaller children aboard were very busy getting drinks. Of course all the walkers lurched along, bumping into each other and grabbing hold of the backs of seats to steady themselves.

The cities and towns they passed through presented their least attractive aspects – warehouses, coal yards, run-down housing, slums. After they had covered about three hundred miles they passed through Omaha and the woman Pearl was sitting with got off. When the train moved on again they headed across Nebraska — a very different landscape. There were no trees on the plains. The grass was parched and yellow instead of luxuriant and green as in Iowa. Most of the land was used for grazing livestock. Often the train track was close to the Platte River — a mile wide and an inch deep, some people claimed. Platte actually means "flat." It was a name well-chosen for this river since it did not have the steep banks or river bluffs often seen along Iowa rivers.

Pearl was glad when it was evening so she could go to the dining car. Dining there was an experience. The food was excellent; the tables were set attractively with fresh table-cloths. On each table there was a flower in a bud vase. The car was paneled with gleaming mahogany. The head waiter seated diners ceremoniously.

The waiter presented a menu that offered the best of everything, including fresh fruit in season. Diners were served with a pleasant flourish by black waiters proud of their expertise. The food was served in covered silver dishes to keep it warm. At the end of the meal a finger bowl was offered so patrons could dip their fingers in it and dry them on the cloth napkin. Pearl lingered, thoroughly enjoying the delicious dinner. When she returned to her coach once more she had to lurch through several cars crowded with strangers. The stares of passengers who had nothing better to do than to size up everyone who traversed the cars discomfited her.

Going between the cars was scary. Here the strong currents of outdoor air and the noise of the wheels, the creaking and groaning of the cars made her anxious to pull open the heavy door and get inside to comparative safety.

Once she was safely ensconced in her seat she took out a book, turned on a dim light, and began to read. She was lost in the book for several hours. Then the conductor turned off all the overhead lights. A man came through the coach renting pillows. Pearl rented one but couldn't get comfortable enough to go to sleep. The night was very long. She wished that she were already with Marie. She would see Ruth too; Ruth was attending summer school at the University of Wyoming. Laramie was within easy driving distance of the homestead, and Ruth had a car.

It seemed strange and lonely to Pearl to be in a family of three. Her early childhood had been spent in a household of thirteen, including her paternal grandfather and her two nieces, Evelyn and Arlynn. Just last year Arlynn had gone to Wyoming to live with her mother. The others had all been gone for some time.

Two were dead. Her grandfather's death was her first experience with death. She would never again hear him read *Uncle Remus*. She wouldn't hear him tell the story of how he and eleven brothers and three sisters emigrated from England to seek opportunities in America where destiny was not determined by one's "station in life." She wouldn't be able to watch him create oil paintings. No more would she hear stories of the Civil War. He had played in a military band. He was at the siege of Vicksburg and made sketches of the camp there. Pearl had gone with her parents to Clinton, Iowa to attend his military funeral. The shot fired into the air by uniformed men startled her but seemed a fitting end to the life of a veteran of that long ago war.

She remembered hearing a lot of talk about another dreadful war that started in Europe when she was only four years old. Stories of atrocities committed by German soldiers in Belgium haunted her dreams. President Wilson, reelected because "he kept us out of war," finally decided the U.S. had to fight along with the Allies. Her brother Herbert immediately enlisted in the army. He had been working in the post office in Mt. Vernon. He was an indefatigable gardener, raising many vegetables, enough to feed the large family in the summer, and plenty to can for winter use.

Soon after this the family moved to Cedar Rapids. She was in second grade at the time.

Brother Earl, who was studying electrical engineering at the University of Iowa, enlisted in the R.O.T.C. He worked nights tending the dynamo that ran the interurban between Iowa City and Cedar Rapids. Between his studies, R.O.T.C. drill and working nights, he didn't get enough rest. His health was undermined. The influenza epidemic of 1918, which took twenty million lives worldwide, caused his death. He had been advised to go to a place with a sunnier, drier climate because he had tuberculosis. On the way to Marie's homestead in Wyoming he had come down with the flu which developed into pneumonia. He was taken to a hospital where he died. At this time Edna also had influenza and pneumonia. Two doctors had given up on her, but her mother nursed her so devotedly that she pulled through. Pearl remembered the grief over Earl's death and the relief the family felt over Edna's recovery.

That same year the Armistice was signed and the family rejoiced that Herbert, who was on a troop ship in New York harbor, would not be sent to the trenches in France. When he returned home, he resumed work and soon married. Pearl went with her parents to the first wedding she had ever attended.

One by one her sisters left home. Edna went to college. Phebe went to Wyoming and met the man she soon married. Ruth took a country school in Wyoming. Betty went to college. Arlynn left to live with her mother.

Life was so different now. Her parents were getting old. Her father wasn't too well. It would be good to be in a livelier place for the summer.

Pearl dozed now and then, only to be thrown off balance when the train jarred to a stop or began its jerky start. If only she had had enough money for the first class ticket needed to reserve a Pullman berth. Then she could have stretched out and slept. She spent some of the sleepless hours dreaming of the homestead and trying to imagine how she and Evelyn would tame wild ponies. She thought too about the surprise Evelyn had mentioned and tried to guess what it was.

When morning finally came everyone looked tired and disheveled while they waited their turn to go wash up, brush their teeth, and comb their hair. Everyone was glad the night was over. There was more lunching, lurching up and down the aisles, and visiting. Pearl had found a railroad timetable with a map of their route and impatiently checked off each town as the train reached it. It seemed to her that the train was just inching along.

The trip finally ended. The train rolled into the station at Cheyenne. There Marie's good friends, Mr. and Mrs. Dunn and their daughter Christine, who was a year or so younger than Pearl, met her and stayed with her until the train to Altus arrived. Christine was excited when she heard about Evelyn's plans for the summer. Her parents promised to bring her to the homestead soon for a visit.

The train arrived and Pearl began the last leg of her journey.

3. The Arrival and the Surprise

The train was at Altus. Excitement! Pearl peered out the window and saw her sister and the children. Marie and five-year-old Jackie were in a two-wheeled cart, and the girls were on horseback. There was no station at Altus; there was no town either. It was a flag stop. There was a one-room school house with a small barn behind it for the teacher's and pupils' horses. There was a house for the section foreman's family, and there were boxcars for the section hands' families.

Altus was about two miles from the homestead. Pearl hurried to get off the train. Marie and Jackie got out of the cart, and the girls dismounted. Everyone hugged and kissed her. There was a lot of excited chatter as her trunk was unloaded from the baggage car and lifted onto the cart. Pearl patted all the horses, then she got into the cart and rode home with Marie and Jackie. She relayed messages from her mother and father as they jogged along. Evelyn and Arlynn rode alongside, listening and asking questions.

"Pearl, would you like to drive the team?" Marie asked.

"Sure, I'd love to." Pearl took the reins and enjoyed the feel of them in her hands. Babe and Dolly trotted along steadily, glad to be on the homeward journey.

The strong Wyoming wind blew her hair every which way. The air was fresh and light. She loved this wind. It gave her a sense of freedom, wildness even, which she always associated with Wyoming. Ahead and behind her the sky met the flat earth. On her left it outlined the crests of a row of round hills, the hogbacks. On her right it defined the tops of the breaks. There were no trees or houses to diminish the immensity of the sky.

"Marie, can Evelyn and I go to see Mr. Farthing tomorrow morning to talk about breaking ponies and get started at once?"

"You must wait at least a week. You have to get used to riding. It will be a long ride to the Farthing ranch. Finding and running in the ponies will mean another long ride, and a fast one. You'll get saddle sores if you take such long rides at once." Grown-ups never want to do things right away, Pearl thought. It is easy for them to postpone things and hard for young people. She knew her sister was right though. She was tired from her train trip. Anyway she could have a lot of fun in the meantime.

When they got to the homestead Evelyn said, "Open the door, Pearl, and you'll see the big surprise." There was a pony colt in the room that served as living room, dining room and kitchen! It might be better to say a "little" surprise, because this was a Shetland colt, very tiny, about two feet tall. It was grey with black and white mane and tail and still had fluffy, light-grey baby hair. Evelyn said, "She's named Orphan. I found her on a cold March day when on a horseback trip into the hills. She was weak and shivering, standing beside a dead mare. I knew a newborn colt couldn't live without its mother's milk, so I picked up the skinny little thing and put her across my saddle."

Marie said, "I prepared some rich warm milk and fed her from a bottle. Sometimes I mixed an egg in her milk. She soon filled out and gained strength. We notified the Farthings, but they haven't come after her. Raising a colt on a bottle is a lot of trouble."

Since she had no mother to stay beside, Orphan liked to be near any human being who was available. She was kept in the house most of the time at first. Thus it became a habit for her to stay indoors part of the day. She was housebroken and would go to the door and paw at the board floor with her tiny hooves when she wanted to go outside.

She like to be groomed. When the children used the curry comb on her, she would turn around after a while and present the other side. She was gradually losing her baby hair, and you could see that she would be a very dark grey with white spots. Marie had read about Shetland ponies. She told the children that they originated in the Shetland or Zetland Islands, the farthest northern islands belonging to Scotland. Here the icy waters of the North Sea mingled with the waters of the North Atlantic. In the winter the ponies grow thick coats about two inches long to protect them from the cold. These ponies are very strong and sure-footed. They live thirty or forty years. The smallest ones are only twenty-four inches tall when full grown.

Orphan was trained to lead. Very young visiting children could sit on her back while she was led about the yard. She wouldn't be strong enough for anyone bigger until she was at least two years old.

She was also spoiled and not too trustworthy. One time she nipped Pearl on the thigh while Pearl was grooming her. The bite was very painful. But everyone loved Orphan and put up with her sulky ways. She was just a spoiled baby and was treated like one.

4. The Homestead

Marie called her house a "tar-paper shack." With only one thousand dollars for a start on homesteading a simple structure was all she could afford. She had to use some of the money for cattle, horses and supplies. On the treeless plains lumber was expensive, and it had to be hauled a long way. So the shack was a flat-roofed building with an entry-way that stretched across the front. Instead of siding, there was tar paper secured with laths. There was one fairly large room, and a bedroom behind that. There was a stove for cooking and heating. The floors were unfinished boards. There was an outhouse in back of the house.

There was another structure nearby – a simple, rectangular building that Marie bought and moved onto her place later. This was dubbed the "apartment" by the girls. It was their bedroom. They could stay up late and read or play games by lamplight. They could tell stories and giggle and laugh as late as they wanted to.

There were three corrals on the place. One small square one was close to the house, and there was a larger square corral with a round corral behind it at some distance from the house. They were made of the slender trunks of quaking aspen trees. Near the house was a chicken house. There was a little shop built against one wall of the chicken house. This had been Jack's blacksmith shop. A pig pen was behind that.

A very important structure was the storm cellar that Jack had dug. It was close to the house. If a tornado struck, the flimsy house would be destroyed. The storm cellar would provide a safe haven.

It looked like a grass-covered mound of earth. There were double doors lying against one side of the mound. When you opened these you could see steps leading to another door, this one upright. Inside this door was a kind of cave with shelves built into three sides. It was cool down there. It smelled earthy, but it was dry. Large cream cans were lined up on the floor. Home-canned goods were neatly arranged on the shelves. Eggs, butter, and all things requiring coolness were stored here. In the winter, food stored here would not freeze.

Marie had ten horses; Dolly and Babe, the work team; Smokey, Baldy, and Headlight, large riding horses; Waltina, Tiny and Pal, smaller horses; and Blackie and Orphan, little ponies. The children could all ride Baldy and Headlight. Baldy was a black mare with a white face. Pearl often rode her. Headlight was a chestnut gelding. He was Marie's horse. Smoky was a big, dapple-grey gelding with a Roman nose. He had been Jack's horse. He was often unmanageable. Pearl stopped riding him after an experience she had with him one summer. He was trotting down the road and suddenly started bucking. She sailed over his ears to a hard landing on the road. Marie rode him; he didn't throw her. He was always ridden with a spade bit. A spade bit has a flat piece of metal that presses on the horse's tongue when you pull in the reins. If the horse is obedient, you keep a very light hand. Snaffle bits – very easy, jointed ones – or bar bits were used on the other horses. Waltina, Tiny and Pal were the favorite mounts of Evelyn and Pearl. They were lively and liked to run.

Marie had fifteen milk cows and some steers and calves. She had started with only a few animals. All the horses and cattle were branded with her registered brand, the Box Cross.

This is the invariable way of determining ownership of stock in Wyoming.

Marie raised chickens and a few pigs. She had a good garden down in the draw, close to the house. Meat, milk, and eggs were plentiful. She bought very little food – mainly flour, sugar, and salt. She sold cream and eggs and marketed steers to get money for necessary purchases including chicken feed, cottonseed cake, and hay. Wild rabbits, both cottontails and jack rabbits, were abundant and provided a change from beef, pork, and chicken. Venison was cold-packed in the hunting season and lasted the year-round. When the family went up into the hills to picnic or to gather wood, they went fishing in the ice-cold rushing mountain streams. If they were lucky they had rainbow trout to eat.

Kerosene lamps and a gas lamp with mantles provided light; wood was used for cooking fuel and heat. They got some of the wood up in the hills. Also old railroad ties were hauled in and cut up. A well with a pump was close to the front of the house.

Homesteaders were not welcomed by the ranchers. Before government lands were claimed by homesteaders, they were available for the ranchers' cattle. The ranchers did not have to fence their land at that time. Their cattle ranged over wide areas. Once a year they had a big round-up when calves were branded and the males were castrated. The ranchers bought purebred bulls to breed the cows. Marie's claim was surrounded by the Farthing ranch. When the claim was fenced off it meant not only the loss of grazing lands but also of a good water hole, the water-filled buffalo wallow and some springs in the draw.

Wars between the homesteaders and ranchers were common a few decades before Marie settled in Wyoming. They were remembered still and tales of them were often told. There had been shootings and arson, and accusations of cattle rustling on both sides of the conflict. Now this was over. Ranchers had fenced their land after barbed wire was invented. Most homesteaders soon discovered that they could not make a living on their small claims and sold out cheaply to the ranchers. The ranchers learned to wait patiently until this occurred.

The ranchers were kind to Marie, a woman alone except for her small daughter. Mr. Farthing gave Evelyn a beautiful little Shetland pony which she called Blackie. Women were scarce in early Wyoming and were treated with special gallantry. Wyoming is called "The Equality State" because it gave women the right to vote in state elections in 1869 when it was still a territory. When it entered the Union, Wyoming authorities were told that this law must be rescinded. Wyoming refused to become a state under that condition. They said that women had shared the hardships of pioneering side by side with men and deserved the right to vote. Finally, Wyoming was allowed to keep women's suffrage for state elections.

Marie was a pioneer woman. She would have been equal to the ordeal of crossing the plains in a covered wagon. She was strong, patient, resourceful, and intelligent. She should have gone to college. She loved books and learning. However, if she had taken this path, it would have denied her the challenge she faced as a young woman in her twenties homesteading alone in the West. She loved life there.

Watching her as she went about her daily chores was a lesson in how work should be done. She never hurried. She took her time and did everything well. She became absorbed in each task and enjoyed it. Nervous energy is energy wasted. It amounts to fighting work instead of doing it efficiently.

Marie baked delicious bread and pastries in the oven of the wood-burning stone. She cold-packed meat and vegetables for the winter. She learned how to deliver foals and calves when there were difficulties. She could treat many animal ailments. There was no veterinarian nearby, no phone and no money to pay fees.

Marie didn't buy chicks to raise. She watched for a hen that would be a good setting hen and put eggs in her nest. In due time tiny yellow, fluffy chicks would hatch out. Then you would see them following the hen as she strutted slowly along, clucking to the chicks to keep them close to her. Marie raised Rhode Island Red chickens. They weren't fenced in, but they always stayed near their feed and water. Chickens often seem to be singularly unintelligent, but sometimes they show good sense. This was the case when a hawk hovered overhead. Pearl was pleased to see how the mother hen would urgently call the chicks to her, spread her wings wide, and shelter the chicks under her body. If she was close to the wagon or anything that would provide shelter from a sky-diving hawk, she would herd the chicks under it.

A description of the homestead wouldn't be complete without including the general setting. The buildings and corrals were on a flat, treeless plain. The grasses on the plain were sparse bunch grass, small bunches of faded grass growing several inches apart; there was also some buffalo grass topped with reddish tufts. Patches of tumbleweed, sagebrush, and prickly pear cactus dotted the prairie. The ground, plainly visible because of the sparse vegetation, was whitish. It was unyielding to the foot — almost cement-like. The contrast to the rich, black loam, abundant trees and lush vegetation in Iowa couldn't have been greater.

Near the house was the huge draw. This draw ran through the homestead and many miles beyond. It was about thirty feet deep and very wide in some places. The draw was not just a single deep canyon. It twisted and turned, and there were many smaller water-carved gullies and channels leading into it. In these there were interesting shapes sculptured by the wind and rain. The children loved to explore these winding passages.

The draw was important. There was a fine spring at the bottom of the draw near the house. A basin was scooped out in the clay, and this had been the source of household water until Jack drilled a well. A water hole elsewhere on the homestead and a large buffalo wallow provided water for the stock.

Marie did the washing in the draw. A circle of stones was used to hold the washtub above a wood fire. After the water was heated, the clothes were scrubbed on a washboard. White things were boiled in a copper boiler. After everything was washed and rinsed, the children carried the washing to the clotheslines by the house. It dried in minutes in the wind and sun.

In some places large deposits of silt had built up in flat planes on the floor of the draw. The vegetable garden was planted on one of these that was across from the spring. It was surrounded by a barbed wire fence to keep out the livestock. The garden provided wonderful vegetables. Marie grew many flowers too.

Surprisingly the whitish soil of Wyoming is fertile. It has many mineral nutriments. All that is needed for growing crops is water. When the garden got too dry the family carried water from the spring to irrigate it.

The grass that is so sparse is wonderfully nutritious. The cattle and horses subsisting on just this grass are sleek and fat. Even in the winter they can find dried grass. The wind sweeps the snow away from the plains rapidly. The cattle need hay only in a harsh winter when it is extremely cold and when the snow is very deep.

 The homestead was eight miles away from the nearest ranch, the Inness ranch near Horse Creek. Horse Creek wasn't a town. There was just a small store there. The storekeepers lived in rooms built onto the back of the store. In the opposite direction, six miles from the homestead, was Iron Mountain where they got their mail. The Farthings' handsome son, Tom, and his beautiful wife, Irene, ran the store and lived behind it too. This was the only building except for a large barn. There was no mountain at Iron Mountain and no iron either. No one seemed to know how it got its name. Cheyenne, which was about thirty-five miles from the homestead, was the nearest city.

5. Life on the Homestead

Pearl woke up early when she heard Evelyn stirring. It was cold. They dressed and put on warm jackets and set out to find the horses. They carried bridles and pans of oats. When they got near the horses they shook the pans so the oats would swish around. Holding the bridles behind their backs they waited until Baldy and Tiny came to them and started eating. Then they looped the reins around their necks and pulled the bridles over their heads and against their teeth until the bits slipped into their mouths. They mounted and set out to find the milk cows. Riding bareback Pearl felt one with the horse. This was more comfortable for the horse than having a thick saddle blanket and heavy saddle fastened tightly around its belly. When riding on the homestead the girls seldom used saddles.

When they located the cows, they slowed to a walk. The cows knew it was milking time and started plodding toward home. Milk cows must not be hurried. Marie, Evelyn, and Pearl each milked five cows. One was one-half Jersey and some were one-fourth Jersey. These were the best milk cows. They were descendants of a Jersey cow Marie bought when she started her homestead. The first calf the Jersey had was called Welcome, because Marie was so happy that it was a heifer. Jersey cows are too delicate for the rigors of Wyoming winters so the cow did not live long. Herefords and Shorthorns are breeds sturdier in build and better adapted to the cold. The Herefords are often called "white face" cattle. They have curly white hair on their faces and along the top of their necks and on their undersides. Otherwise they are a deep reddish color. The Shorthorns were reddish and white with many roan speckles among the white parts. These were the breeds that, mixed with the Jersey strain, made Marie's cows strong enough to withstand the harsh Wyoming winters.

They milked at the same times each day and each person always milked the same five cows. Cows give down their milk more readily if they are milked on schedule and are used to the person who milks them.

Each cow was different in its ways. Some were nervous, others calm. Some would kick over the pail. Others were expert at switching their tails into the milker's face. Pearl liked the cows and enjoyed the milking chores. When she petted their faces she noticed that their breath smelled like new-mown hay. She would sit on a low stool, lean her head against the cow's flank and begin milking rhythmically. At first the jets of milk pinged against the pail; then as the pail began to fill, they made a softer sound in the foamy milk.

Often Socks, the handsome black cat with four white feet and a white tie under his chin, came by. He looked as though he were in formal attire. Stately as he appeared, he enjoyed a milking-time game. If a thin stream of milk was directed toward him, he would try to catch it in his mouth. When he had had enough, he began the job of grooming himself, dampening a paw with his raspy tongue and rubbing it against his fur. Pearl thought it strange that such fastidious animals as cats enjoy this messy game of catch. She knew that many farm and ranch cats do enjoy it even though they have dishes of milk they could lap up neatly.

All the milk had to be carried into the house. It was strained through a cloth and some whole milk was bottled for home use and to sell to the Mexicans at Altus.

Then the rest of it was poured into the large bowl atop the separator which was located in the entry way. When the crank was turned the milk went through a stack of discs which revolved very fast. This separated the cream from the milk. The cream came out of one spout and the skim milk from another. The cream was stored in cans about two feet high which were kept in the storm cellar until sold.

Some of the whole milk was fed to the calves. They had been weaned by the time Pearl arrived. At feeding time Marie put the calves in the corral nearest the house. They stuck their heads between the poles and drank eagerly from the pails of milk. If you tried to feed them outside the corral they would butt their heads against the pail and spill the milk. Pearl thought it was fun to feed them. They were so cute. The white hair on their faces was curly. Their little bodies and spraddled legs were slight. As they noisily sucked in the warm milk, their stomachs rounded out. When they had had enough, the frothy milk dripped from their muzzles. Cottonseed cake was provided for them too. After the feeding they were turned loose so they could wander and graze at will.

Other chores were gathering the eggs and feeding the chickens. Cracked corn was scattered on the ground for the chickens. They hurried about pecking at it. They got milk to drink as well as water. There was much skim milk and little use for it except occasionally to make some cottage cheese. Even the pigs got skim milk.

If the hens were on the nest Pearl was a little afraid to reach under them for the eggs. They would ruffle their feathers and squawk angrily, threatening to peck the hand so rudely disturbing them. Sometimes they really did peck.

Pearl seldom fed the pigs. She disliked them. They

were disgusting, she thought, snorting and grunting, gulping their swill. They smelled awful too. Marie liked them and said that they were intelligent. She said that scientific experiments have proven this to be a fact. They are smarter than horses or dogs. Also they are not really dirty animals. If given a chance, they like to keep clean. It is true that they like mud and will cool themselves in it. But mud is not filth.

Another chore was churning butter. They did this in a glass churner. The cover had a beater fastened beneath it. Someone had to turn the wheel until tiny globules of butter separated from the bluish whey. Then the bits of butter were strained from the buttermilk, rinsed with cold water and put in a shallow wooden bowl. A flat wooden paddle was used to "work" the butter. This meant pressing it against the bowl until all the buttermilk was worked out of it. Then salt was added and it was stored in a container. This butter was sweet and delicious, especially when spread on bread fresh from the oven.

Jackie loved butter. Sometimes he would eat it by the spoonful. So the girls tried to get him interested in turning the churn. Very soon his arm would begin to hurt. It was boring to keep turning and turning the beater. He would dash outdoors to play with his wagon, his pony, and his dog, Dirk, his arm miraculously healed.

The girls had to keep the large wood box by the kitchen stove filled. This meant sawing wood with a crosscut saw. The wood was placed over sawhorses. The crosscut saw was long with a handle at each end. Two people worked it, pushing and pulling in rhythm. When the wood was cut into stove-size lengths, it was stood on end and split with an axe. Sometimes because of knots in the wood it was necessary to use a wedge.

Providing kindling was another chore. This meant collecting wood chips and tiny splinters of wood that had fallen on the ground.

Sometimes the girls helped Marie with the housework, doing dishes, sweeping and scrubbing the floor, polishing the kitchen stove, carrying out the ashes. In the evening Pearl or Evelyn went after the cows again and repeated all the chores. These chores were interesting to Pearl, because she liked animals. Also life on the homestead had the charm of novelty for her.

6. Exploring

One morning after the chores were finished, Evelyn said to Pearl, "Let's pack a lunch and go on a long ride. We haven't ridden very far since you came."

"Yes, let's ride up into the breaks and explore. I'll ride Tiny."

"I'll ride Waltina. We'll give the slip to Arlynn and Jackie. If we go down into the draw and ride fast up to the breaks and take a few turns up there between the hills they'll never find us."

Tiny was not a pony, but he wasn't as big as a horse either. He was a dark bay with black mane and tail. He was beautifully built, like a small thoroughbred horse. Pearl liked to ride Tiny, because he was spirited and willing to gallop.

Waltina was a beautiful small black mare. She was given to Evelyn by Walt Talbott, a rancher, hence her unusual name. Waltina liked to run too. She also had a wonderful gait called singlefooting which gave her rider the sensation of being gently rocked. It was much more pleasant than the repeated jolts from a trotting horse.

The girls packed a small lunch and set out. Arlynn and Jackie tried to follow them as usual but were soon left far behind. Evelyn said, "Let's go up on the prairie now."

The horses scrambled up the steep side of the draw. The girls rode on at a walk. They saw a prairie dog town and rode toward it. Alerted by the thud of the horses' hooves the little animals, more than twice the size of a squirrel, chubby, with round heads and tiny ears, popped out of their burrows and sat upright near the openings. They noisily chattered warnings to one another. When the riders came too near, they whisked into the safety of their homes. These are interconnected by tunnels so the prairie dogs can disappear into one and pop up out of one farther away. This was a large prairie dog town with dozens of burrows.

"Pearl, the cowboys say that coyotes hunt in pairs when they are after prairie dogs. One lopes through the town, paying no attention to the dwellers. When he has passed several burrows, the little animals reappear to watch him depart. Then the second coyote rushes in and pounces on one."

They saw a badger. It was about two feet long and had beautiful thick tan fur with black stripes on its head. Its legs were very short. Badgers are burrowing animals and dig their homes in the ground. Riders must be watchful of these, because a running horse can easily break a leg stepping into a badger hole. A horse with a broken leg must be shot. A rider could also be killed by being thrown from a horse that steps into a badger hole.

They saw a little prairie owl sitting atop a burrow. These owls find an old burrow to live in since they cannot dig.

Pearl liked the sage brush and tumbleweeds. The sage brush was a sort of silver-grey. It had a pungent odor. Tumbleweeds dry up in the autumn; then the leafless stems, which together form a roundish shape, break loose and go rolling across the flat plains for months.

Prickly pear cacti were everywhere. Their delicate, waxy flowers were beautiful, yellow, orange, and red-orange.

Many tiny wildflowers dotted the landscape. Among

these were black-eyed daisies and lupine.

They rode to the top of a hill where there were several circles of stones. Here Indians had camped. The girls dismounted, and while Tiny and Waltina grazed they knelt and looked for pieces of stone which had been used to make arrowheads. There were many of these from which flakes had been skillfully struck. These stones were not like the others in the breaks. The Indians must have brought them there. The girls each put a few of these into their pockets.

"Evelyn, did you ever try to chip stones like these with other stones?"

"No. Let's try it now."

They selected some stones and tried again and again to strike flakes from them with no luck.

"The Indians must have some special tools." Evelyn remarked.

"Even if they did, it would have taken a lot of skill and a lot of patience to strike off flakes in such a way as to make an arrow with a point sharp enough to penetrate a buffalo's hide, and with those two little flaring projections at the top," Pearl commented. "Evelyn, you have found several perfect arrowheads. Will you give one to me?"

"Yes, I will unless you find one yourself. Let's come up here and camp several days, Pearl. There's a spring in that little cave near here. Remember?"

"Oh, I want to do that. I think Marie will let us, don't you?"

"I think she will. Let's go get a drink from the spring now."

They led their mounts down to the cave and got a drink. After they ate their lunch, sitting in the shade of the cave, they rode around in the breaks.

"I have an idea. Why don't we go down to the buffalo wallow and ride through it? It's getting hot and that would cool off our horses," Evelyn suggested. "There are frogs there. Maybe we can catch some for supper."

"I've never eaten frogs, Evelyn."

"You just eat the legs. They taste a little like chicken. They're good!"

"Well, I have read that they eat them in France and think they are a real treat. I guess I'd try them."

The girls rode down the draw toward the buffalo wallow, keeping out of sight of the house. They came to an overhanging wall of the draw where swallows had built their mud nests. Evelyn proceeded to throw rocks at the nests, breaking them down. Many had eggs in them. Pearl wouldn't take part in this. She tried to get Evelyn to stop, but Evelyn wouldn't. She said the swallows carried diseases. Pearl felt sad when she thought how the nests had been laboriously built of tiny globules of mud. They were skillfully and neatly built right against the mud wall of the draw. Each nest had a small round hole for an entrance.

"Evelyn, let's go on now to the buffalo wallow." Pearl began riding on. Evelyn followed her.

They smelled the fragrance of wild roses growing in the draw. The cries of the killdeer alerted them to the presence of these birds which liked to frequent the part of the draw where water oozed out of the sandy bottom. They could imagine that the birds were saying, "Kill deer, kill deer." The chirping was a cheerful sound despite the dire message.

Later when they were emerging from the draw a safe distance from the house, where they hoped Arlynn and Jackie wouldn't see them, they saw a lovely bluebird. It was a light powder blue with an orange-red breast, a western bluebird. These were not common around the homestead. The girls were impressed by its beauty and hoped it would nest on the homestead.

When they reached the buffalo wallow, a big shallow pond, they rode through it repeatedly. In the middle it was deep enough so the horses had to swim for a few yards. They seemed to enjoy the water. Just as they entered the water for one final crossing, Waltina started to lie down. Evelyn jumped off, and Waltina rolled over in the water.

Pearl couldn't help laughing. Evelyn was angry at Waltina and grabbed the reins, led her to dry ground, got on, and whipped her with the ends of the reins. Yelling and kicking her sides at the same time, she rode her fast through the pond. Then she repeated the performance, returning to where Pearl was waiting.

"I forgot. She always wants to roll in the water. I have to teach her not to do that." Evelyn jumped down and waded into the water to hunt frogs. She didn't ask Pearl to help. Evelyn had no difficulty in catching the frogs. She killed each one as soon as she caught it and tossed it onto the grass. When she had seven or eight of them she said, "That's enough. Let's take them home."

Marie was glad to get the frogs. She fried the legs for supper. They were tasty. The pigs got the rest of the frog meat.

7. Milk Merchants

Evelyn and Pearl made some money selling milk to the railroad section hands at Altus. The railroad ran parallel to one side of the homestead, not far beyond the fence. The section crew was made up entirely of immigrants from Mexico. They spoke Spanish and understood very little English. Their foreman, an American, and his family lived at Altus too.

These workers were responsible for repairing the track, ensuring the safety of the passengers and train crew. They earned very little for this important work. They had few possessions and had no cars or horses. They used a hand car to go to the work sites and to go to Iron Mountain to shop. This hand car had no motor. The men pushed and pulled on a bar to propel it on the tracks.

The men and their wives and children lived in box cars. They were painted a dull, dark red. They had no modern conveniences.

The people were friendly and smiling. Their children were beautiful with their big dark eyes, black shiny hair, and rosy cheeks. They were always dressed in bright colored clothes.

The parents were glad to buy milk for the little ones. Each day after the evening milking the girls rode there, carrying bottles of milk and picking up the empty bottles. On payday they collected what was owed for that week. It was necessary to collect on pay days. When the men went to Iron Mountain to do their weekly grocery shopping, they had to spend most of their money. Some people said that after they bought the week's necessities, they gambled.

One time they bought bright pink and red scarves for Pearl and Evelyn — gifts of friendship purchased out of meager earnings. The girls tied these around their necks and felt like rodeo cowgirls.

One evening when they went to Altus for the usual evening delivery, no smiling faces greeted them. Most of the people were indoors, and they could hear sounds of weeping coming from one boxcar. The girls gave the milk to one man who was standing outside.

"What is the matter? Why are people crying?" Pearl asked.

The man started to answer in a flood of Spanish, then remembered and spoke in broken English, "Little girl. Snake bite."

"Which little girl? Will she be all right?" Evelyn questioned.

"Rosa. Four years." The man held his hand parallel to the ground indicating how small Rosa was. "Dead. Bite here." The man pointed to his cheek.

The girls were shocked and saddened. They knew they should go inside and say something to the parents, but they didn't know what to say. They wanted to go home.

Finally Pearl said, "Let's go in." They went into the boxcar house shyly and approached the mother. Evelyn patted the mother's shoulders. Pearl held one of her hands. All they could get out of their aching throats was the word, "Sorry. Sorry."

When they went outside again the section foreman came over to tell them what had happened. "Rosa was picking flowers when the snake struck her. She was leaning over, and that is why it struck her on the cheek. She was the only child of this couple."

They rode home and told Marie. She said, "Usually a rattlesnake bite will not kill a person, if they don't panic and run, spreading the poison throughout their blood. And if the bite is cut and the poison sucked out. Did they do that?"

"We don't know. We didn't ask any questions. We were so shocked we couldn't think. Anyway they can't speak English very well," Pearl said.

"A bite on the cheek would be particularly dangerous," Marie said. "It's so close to the brain. If only we had a doctor out here."

"I wonder if they found the snake," Evelyn said. "There are probably two of them. I think I should go back and look for them."

"Evelyn," Pearl said. "Remember, we saw two men walking along the tracks. I bet they were looking for the snake."

"All the men will search for the snake," Marie assured them.

"They'll find it and kill it. I hope they find two of them," Evelyn said with satisfaction.

8. The Pony Deal

"Marie, I've been here five days already," Pearl remarked one afternoon. Her sister was mixing a large batch of bread dough. Later in the day the smell of newly-baked bread would draw everyone to the kitchen. Soon they would be biting through the crisp crusts of thick slices spread with fresh butter.

"Yes, you came Sunday," she answered noncommittally.

"I've been riding for hours every day. I haven't felt any stiffness since the second day. I feel rested and strong."

Marie began to laugh. "I can guess why I am getting this information about the passage of time and about your physical condition. You want to start the pony training project. Right?"

Pearl laughed too. "Yes, you guessed. We want to ride over to the Farthing ranch today and see if we can make a deal with him."

"In the morning, Pearl. If he agrees to let you run in some ponies to break, you'll probably want to ride up into the hills and bring them back after talking to him. It will take time to locate the ponies, and it will be a long, hard ride running them in."

Pearl gave her sister a hug and a kiss. "I know you're right. Thanks for letting us go tomorrow." Pearl ran outside to find Evelyn and tell her the good news.

"Good! I'll ride Waltina and you ride Tiny. They are fast runners. Let's go right after the chores are done in the morning. Maybe Arlynn will agree to feed the calves and chickens and pigs and gather the eggs. Then we can leave right after milking."

Arlynn agreed to help in this way. Marie said that she would run the separator and take care of the milk and cream. Evelyn had a new idea. "Why don't we make it part of the bargain that we will keep one pony for Arlynn. We'll find one that's larger, because she's growing fast. She doesn't have her own horse, because she hasn't been living here with us very long."

"That's a great idea! Let's go find her and tell her."

Arlynn was excited. "Can I choose the one I want? I want to go with you."

"We'll ask Mr. Farthing if you can choose the one you want. You must stay here and help mother. When you see us coming with the ponies, fasten the gate of the corral open. Then go back to the house so the ponies won't be afraid to go in," Evelyn said.

"Okay. I'll be watching. And I'll choose my pony the minute they are shut in the corral. Will you break it for riding first of all?"

"We will," they assured her.

The girls went to bed early that night so they would be well rested. They woke up before the alarm rang and hurried out to catch Tiny and Waltina and bring in the cows. When the milking was finished they carried the milk to the house, ate a big breakfast and hurried out to saddle their horses. The horses always took a deep breath and held it when the cinch was about to be fastened. The girls had to slip it through the ring and hold it, waiting until the horses had to exhale. Then they would quickly pull on it 'til it was taut and securely fasten it so the saddle wouldn't slip.

They gave the horses a drink from a pail and took a drink of the cool well water themselves and then set off at a leisurely pace. They would walk and trot all the way to the ranch, about eight miles away. When they found the ponies, the horses would need all their wind and strength to cut them from the band and drive them in.

The ride was uneventful. Pearl and Evelyn excitedly discussed the way they would train the ponies. Eight or ten would be all they could train in the summer months, they decided.

They stopped at the Iron Mountain store to visit a while with Tom and Irene Farthing. Tom and Irene were special friends of Ruth's. The first year she taught in Wyoming she spent many weekends with them. She was a welcome visitor at the Farthing ranch, too. The Farthings made the year very pleasant for her.

Evelyn and Pearl bought some snacks and got a drink there and told them where they were going and what they wanted to do.

"Dad will be very much interested. Most people want a pony that is trained," Tom assured them. "I hope you make a good bargain."

When they arrived at the ranch they were received hospitably and given some refreshments. After some conversation about Ruth and Marie, Pearl said, "We have come here on business, Mr. Farthing. We would like to make a deal with you to break some ponies."

"I'm interested, girls. How much do you want for each pony you break?"

"We would rough break one for fifteen dollars. Or if you want us to gentle some so small children can ride them, twenty-five dollars each," Evelyn said.

"That sounds fair."

"We would like to keep one pony for my sister as part of the deal."

"That's okay. The ponies are worth about fifty dollars unbroken. Let's say you gentle two ponies to pay for the one you keep for your sister. You can choose the one you want. Don't drive in a stallion though. I pay a lot of money for them to bring in new blood.

"We'll be careful not to do that. We thought we could train about eight or ten ponies in the three summer months. Is it all right to take that many?" Pearl asked.

"That's fine! Run in as many as you want."

"We want to get the ponies today," said Evelyn. "Can you tell us where they are most likely to be?"

"Evelyn, you know those ponies run all over the hills. We never know just where they are. But I'll draw you a little map showing some of the places where we have seen them lately while out checking on the cattle. They may not be in any of these places now though." Mr. Farthing had taken an envelope out of his pocket and was making a rough map showing a few landmarks. He handed it to Evelyn and said, "Come out on the porch, and I'll point out the direction you should take and some features of the hills that could roughly guide you."

When he had finished giving them some directions, he said, "I still have my sons' pony buggy and harness. Would you like to make them part of the bargain? Why not come out to the barn and see them?"

They were interested at once. They saw that the buggy and harness were in perfect shape. The buggy was black with red trimming, and the harness was black with shiny metal fittings. "We don't have a pony broken for driving, but we could train one," Evelyn said. "What do you think, Pearl?"

Pearl wanted that pony buggy. Probably every kid wants one. She could imagine driving to Iron Mountain or Horse Creek for supplies. Often it was a problem tying things on the saddles. Several times Tiny had spooked because of the rattling of paper, shied and almost thrown her as she was getting on his back.

"Let's take it!"

"I'll bring it in the truck soon," Mr. Farthing said. "How about counting it in for thirty dollars?"

They sealed the bargain with a handshake. No written contract is necessary when there is mutual trust.

9. Driving in the Ponies

They rode off happy about the deal they had made. Mr. Farthing had treated them like adults, and they felt proud. Evelyn said, "We'll soon be in the business of pony training. Arlynn will have her own pony, and we will have some cash coming to us too."

"We'll surprise everyone with the pony buggy," Pearl replied.

They followed the map faithfully but didn't see any ponies. Then they rode and rode looking other places. "We have to go home, Evelyn," Pearl finally said. "The sun is getting low in the sky. They'll be getting worried about us. If we are up here in the hills at night, we'll get lost. We won't be able to see any landmarks. We can't drive wild ponies in at night."

Evelyn reluctantly agreed, and they started homeward. They rode between two hills toward the plain. All at once they saw a band of ponies, led by a beautiful black and white stallion.

"Pearl, we'll get as near to them as we can. Walk your pony. When we get too close, they'll run. We'll cut about ten out of the band and get them running. Don't let them double back!" Evelyn spoke very low. "I'll watch the right, and you watch the left."

The riders approached slowly. Suddenly the stallion snorted an alarm, whirled and dashed away followed by his band. The girls cantered after them at some distance. The ponies finally slowed from their run, and the girls slowed down too. The ponies were tired and changed to a trot, then to a walk. Evelyn and Pearl followed, keeping the same distance.

"Pearl, let's stop and rest our horses. We'll soon be charging in and cutting out some of the band."

They stopped and let Tiny and Waltina graze. The ponies stopped to rest and graze too, warily watching them.

"Which ones will we try to separate from the others?" Pearl asked.

"We'll try to drive a wedge between those ten or twelve that are over to the left. We may not get them all. The fastest ones will get away from us," Evelyn said.

"Let's dash into the band side by side and cut them off from the rest, and then you keep to the right flank, Evelyn, and I'll keep to the left as you said earlier."

"They'll try their best to rejoin the band. It will be all we can do to force them to move away."

"Are you ready Evelyn? Let's go."

They galloped toward the ponies and drove a wedge between the ones they had selected and the rest of the band. The stallion shrilled a warning and dashed away to lead the ponies to safety. A few of the ponies the girls had cut out escaped and ran to catch up with him. Now they had only nine ponies in the bunch. They too tried desperately to rejoin the band, but Tiny and Waltina darted back and forth skillfully, guided by a rein laid against the right or left side of their necks. Western horses are taught to neck rein. Both reins are held in one hand. This is a quicker signal than pulling on a rein and more pleasant for the horses than a pull on their mouths. Waltina and Tiny hardly needed guidance. They seemed to enjoy the game of heading off the ponies. They were breathing hard, and their coats were lathered with foam, but they did not need urging on.

When the girls spied a fence in the distance, Evelyn sent Pearl ahead to open the gate. Then Pearl circled around to get behind the band again. They maneuvered the bunch toward the gate and through it, then Pearl closed the gate. Now the ponies could not return to the band. The girls hung back to see if the ponies would slow down. They did. The riders zig-zagged back and forth at a walk or a trot and kept them moving toward the homestead.

Marie, Arlynn, and Jackie saw them coming down from the hills, and Arlynn opened the gate to the homestead pasture and the gate to the corral. Then she went inside the house so she would not scare the ponies.

There was a long, barbed-wire wing fence attached to one side of the big corral, so once the animals were driven close enough to the corral there was only one side to guard against a breakaway. The ponies did not want to go into the corral, but they were gradually forced in and the gate was fastened shut.

Marie, Arlynn, and Jackie came out to look them over. "I want that one over there," Arlynn announced, pointing to the largest one, a blood-bay pinto with beautiful white markings and a black mane and tail. "Isn't she pretty? I'm going to call her Merrilegs."

"She has beautiful conformation," Marie commented. "The coloring is unusual, and that bright bay color is really showy. You made a good choice!"

"Break her first, won't you?" Arlynn urged. "I can't wait to ride her."

"I want to ride that little black one," Jackie said. "Let's call it Blackie."

"You already have a pony named Blackie, Jackie. How about calling this one Midnight?" Evelyn suggested.

"Okay, but hurry up and train him. I want another pony to ride."

"Look at that beautiful one that's almost all white,"

Pearl said. "It has just a few golden tan spots and a white mane and tail. I'm naming that one Snowball."

They went on suggesting names and praising the beauty of the little animals. The ponies pranced about on their dainty little hooves, tossing their luxuriant, thick manes and tails. There were two beautiful black and white pintos, another all black pony, and one mostly tan with white spots. Another was mainly white. All the ponies were pretty.

"Some were smaller than we wanted to bring in, Marie," Pearl explained. "But we really couldn't cut out just exactly the ones we wanted."

"You would have had to have a holding corral in the pasture and more riders to do that, Pearl. Anyway, some buyers will want the smallest ones if they are buying them for very small children."

Pearl and Evelyn unsaddled their horses and brushed them down. They were very hot so they could not give them water. They were turned loose to graze. By the time they reached the water hole they would have cooled down.

"Now we'll let all the ponies out of the corral. They must be rested before you begin their training," Marie said. "They'll stay together in the pasture and stay away from the other horses too. Horses don't like strange pasture mates. Our horses will kick and bite them if they come near. The ponies will keep each other company."

"Tomorrow we'll start training Merrilegs," Evelyn said.

"Remember, girls, that these are wild ponies. Everything here is strange and frightening to them. Remember, too, that they will have no idea of what you want them to do. First you must win their confidence. They must accept your presence and learn that you will not hurt them. You must be very patient in teaching them everything, how to lead, to accept a weight on their backs, accept a bit, learn to turn left and right. Patience is the key. You must go slowly."

"Marie, you'll help us won't you? I mean, tell us what to do," Pearl asked.

"Of course, but much of it you can figure out for yourselves."

"I've watched people break horses, Pearl," Evelyn said confidently. "I know how to do it."

10. Breaking Ponies

Pearl and Evelyn had a good rest and got up on schedule to do the chores. After breakfast they drove the ponies into the corral, then let them out a few at a time until only Merrilegs was left. After numerous tries Evelyn dropped a rope around Merrilegs' neck as she circled the round corral. The end of the rope was then looped around the snubbing post in the center of the corral, and slowly and steadily Evelyn pulled the pony close to the pole as it reared and strained to get away. When the pony was close Evelyn gave the end of the rope to Pearl and told her to keep it taut.

After the pony calmed down, Evelyn picked up a gunny sack tied to a short rope. This she tossed onto the pony's back. Merrilegs rolled her eyes 'til the whites shone, and twisted and turned 'til it fell off. The girls took turns putting it on and pulling it off until Merrilegs stood still. Her shuddering skin showed her fear of it, but she didn't move. They moved the sack here and there on her back until she no longer showed any fear. This took time and patience. Eventually they could throw the sack on her back, and she would remain calm. This seemingly senseless procedure called "sacking" accomplished two things: the pony became accustomed to something on her back, and she began to get used to the presence of human beings. The girls spoke to her gently and reassuringly during this process and finally patted her on her neck and back and head. She began to lose her fear of them.

Marie kept reminding the girls that the only time

these ponies had had contact with people before this was when they were rounded up, driven into a branding corral, branded with a hot iron, and, if males, castrated. Maybe they remembered the trauma of the onetime contact. Maybe not. But they were not used to being near people and were afraid.

The next step was to teach Merrilegs to lead. Evelyn put a halter on her and untied her from the post. At first she tried to pull away. Then the pony set her legs apart and would not budge. Speaking to her gently Evelyn pulled her head around to one side and walked away so she would have to move her legs to maintain balance. She took a step or two. With time and patience Evelyn got the pony to follow her as she held the halter rope loosely and walked along. Then Pearl took a turn.

All this training had to be repeated day after day. One day Evelyn said, "Let's put a saddle on her today. She won't mind the saddle blanket, but she won't like the weight of the saddle and the cinch around her belly."

"Remember," Pearl said, "Marie told us we can't ride these wild ponies with a saddle. She's afraid a boot will get caught in a stirrup when we are thrown."

"I know, but the saddle will be something like a person on her back, and we'll turn her loose with it fastened so she'll learn she can't get rid of it. Maybe it will help her get used to carrying a load."

So Evelyn put the saddle blanket on. It was no problem. Then she tried the saddle, but could not get near Merrilegs with it. So she snubbed her to the post and eventually the two girls got the saddle on her and fastened it despite the pony's struggles. Then they turned her loose, and she bucked and reared and plunged wildly about the corral trying to get rid of the frightening and uncomfortable burden. She finally learned that she could not shake it off and stood still, breathing hard. The lead rope was snapped onto the halter, and they took turns leading her around the corral, petting her and speaking to her.

"I wish we could use the saddle. It would be easier to stay on. We could hold onto the saddle horn too," Pearl said. "But I know Marie won't let us until she's tame."

Western saddles offer a lot of support to the rider. They have high swells to fit the thighs. The back of the saddle, or cantle, is high so the rider will not slip off the rump of a rearing horse. The saddle horn is sturdy enough to hold a roped steer.

"Cowboys don't hold onto a saddle horn, Pearl – that's sissy stuff."

"Well, I'm a girl, and I'd hold on. And so would you. A handful of mane isn't much use in staying on a bucking horse."

The girls knew that even with high swells and cantle and with feet braced in the stirrups, a bucking horse can throw a rider in time.

"All we can do is grip the belly with our knees and hang onto the mane," Evelyn said. "We won't try to ride her today though. Let's saddle her for several days and lead her around some more. When we ride her we won't be using the halter, so we should get her used to a bridle, too."

Days later when Merrilegs accepted the saddle calmly, the girls put a bridle on her. This was not easy. She clamped her teeth together firmly. Eventually the pressure of the bit being pulled against her mouth caused it to open, the bit popped in, and the bridle was fastened. Then the girls took turns leading the pony about the corral.

When they took the saddle off, they leaned on her back so she would feel their weight and accept their closeness. They often groomed Merrilegs so she would become accustomed to being touched. They could start other ponies on these slow processes too, because they did not want the session with any one pony to last more than about two hours. They began training Midnight next, to please Jackie.

The day came to ride Merrilegs. The girls were quite sure that she would object violently to a rider, and they knew they could not stay on long without a saddle. So they were prepared to be unseated many times. Fortunately they would not have as far to fall as from a big horse, but the ground was hard and the fall would be jarring. It would take courage to get up and get on again. They would have to do it right away so the pony would learn that resistance was useless.

"Evelyn, when you are thrown, I'll try next. And then you again, okay? That way the shock will wear off a bit," Pearl suggested.

"Okay, but I don't always want to be first. Let's take turns being the first to ride each pony we break."

"That's fair enough. We'll draw lots to see who is first to ride Merrilegs."

Evelyn had to ride first. "Remember, Pearl, when we decide to ride Midnight, you are first."

"I'll remember."

Evelyn mounted Merrilegs with some difficulty as Pearl held her. When the pony was turned loose she bucked hard. Evelyn remained seated for a few jumps and then fell off.

They caught Merrilegs when she quieted down, and Pearl got on her. She did not stay long. Then Evelyn again. Each time the girls waited until Merrilegs was quiet and reassured her by talking to her and petting her on the neck. They understood that she was merely trying to get an unaccustomed, frightening burden off her back. When she was no longer afraid she would stop bucking.

When she stopped throwing her rider, the girls trained her to turn right and left and to stop when they pulled on the reins. They did not need to teach her neck reining. Little children would pull on the right rein to turn right and on the left one to turn left.

The big day came when they opened the corral gate and rode out onto the prairie. They did not know what the reaction to this relative freedom would be. Maybe the pony would be well-behaved; maybe she would act up or run as fast as she could.

Pearl suggested, "Why don't we saddle up Waltina, and one of us ride alongside Merrilegs? Maybe we could even lead her for a while until she gets the idea of how to move along."

"Pearl, you're forgetting that the other horses don't like these ponies. It just wouldn't work. But when we get Merrilegs trained well, maybe we could use her to help train the others. I know Jack used to have Marie ride along with him on Headlight when he was training a bronc."

Pearl was to be the first to ride Merrilegs outside the corral since Evelyn had been first to ride inside the corral. Pearl was frightened as she mounted and rode out into the open. Merrilegs surprised her by moving along at a walk. She was a naturally gentle pony once she got over her fears.

After they were sure she was reliable, Arlynn rode Merrilegs. She was pleased and proud to have her own pony.

After a week or so had passed, Mr. Farthing brought the pony buggy and harness. Marie decided that Tiny, a small horse, would be the best one to train to pull the buggy. He proved to be quite easy to train, and for a while the children enjoyed driving about. But it was not nearly as much fun as riding, and after a while they did not use it very much. They drove to the store sometimes, and when children visited they would get it out for their delight. Riding in a buggy behind a trotting horse was boring. The driver had to make careful turns or the buggy would overturn. There was no feeling of free movement as there was in riding horseback. Then the horse can wheel about in quick turns. It can go up steep hills and slide down abrupt declines. It can run fast. The rider and the horse are one; the horse senses what the rider wants it to do.

One day Pearl said, "I wish we hadn't bargained for the buggy. We don't use it very much. We could have earned more money instead."

Evelyn agreed, "It was a mistake, but maybe we can sell it after a while."

"That's a good idea," Pearl said. "I thought it would be wonderful to drive a pony buggy. It isn't. Sometimes you find out that something you just have to buy is not as wonderful as you imagined it would be."

11. To the Hills for Wood

"We need more wood," Marie remarked one day. "Let's pack up a picnic in the morning, hitch Babe and Dolly to the wagon and head for the hills."

All the cooking was done on the wood-burning kitchen stove, which served also to heat the house on cold mornings and evenings. A lot of wood was needed. There was not a single tree on the homestead. They had to go to the hills several miles away to get firewood. There were many trees there, mostly pines and aspens.

They always enjoyed the day-long excursion that gathering the wood entailed. They would gather the wood; no trees would be cut down. They wanted dry wood, fallen branches. Pine knots were especially good; they kindled quickly and made a hot fire.

Evelyn and Pearl had been working with ponies steadily for many days. They had only two of them trained for riding, Merrilegs and Midnight, and had sacked and halter-broken two more. They were ready for a respite.

Jackie and Arlynn were eager to go too. "I'll ride Midnight," Jackie said. This little pony had proved to be unusually tractable and gentle. Jackie loved to ride him about the yard.

"I'd be lonesome riding in the wagon by myself, Jackie. I need you to help drive the team, too," Marie said. This appeal changed Jackie's mind. Marie knew he would get tired on the long ride and take his usual nap in the back of the wagon. He was such an active little boy that he never had to be put to bed. When he was ready to drop from exhaustion he would get his favorite "piddow," lie down and go to sleep instantly.

"I'll ride Tiny," Arlynn said. "I don't want to use Merrilegs for this long ride."

"I'll ride Waltina," Evelyn announced.

"I'll ride Baldy," Pearl decided.

Marie's picnic lunches were more like gourmet dinners. That night she killed some young frying chickens, fried them a golden brown, made wonderful potato salad and a chocolate cake. She packed homemade rolls, milk and some fresh garden vegetables. They took an old kettle so they could boil coffee.

They turned in early and got up at the break of dawn to bring in the team, the three riding horses and the cows for milking. Evelyn drove in the horses and Pearl brought the cows in more slowly. Evelyn had the horses watered and saddled and bridled by the time Pearl put the cows in the corral. They milked, did the chores and went in to eat a hearty breakfast.

While they were eating breakfast, Dirk began barking furiously. They looked out the doorway and saw the Dunn's old touring car approaching. Nonnie was driving and Christine was with her.

"This is great. Now they can go with us," Marie said.

As the car came to a stop all crowded around and talked at once. "Hello!" "Hello!" "We're glad you're here." "You came just in time to go with us on a picnic in the hills." "Hi, Christine, we'll get a horse for you."

"Are you really breaking ponies, Evelyn and Pearl?" Christine asked. "I can't wait to see them."

"Yes, we are. We have nine of them. Maybe we'll get back early enough to bring them in and work with them awhile," Evelyn said.

"I want you to see my pony, Merrilegs," Arlynn said proudly. "Pearl and Evelyn are gentling two ponies to pay for her. She's the most beautiful one of all."

"Midnight is beautiful too! I can ride Midnight," Jackie exclaimed.

Marie explained that the purpose of the trip to the hills was to get wood. If Nonnie and Christine would rather just stay at the homestead, she could postpone the trip.

"Marie, I think it will be great fun to go on a picnic," Nonnie said. "We can help load up the wagon with wood so you can get back a little earlier."

Just then Orphan came around the corner of the house. Milk was dripping from her mouth.

"Mama, Orphan's been drinking the chickens' milk again," Jackie cried.

"What a darling pony. It's so little. Is this one trained?" Christine asked.

"This isn't one that we are training. Orphan is only a few months old. I found her early this spring standing beside her dead mother."

Marie told them how she had fed the starving colt until it grew strong and healthy.

"She comes in the house with us," Jackie said.

Christine petted Orphan and exclaimed, "She's so tiny and so pretty."

"Come in. We're just finishing breakfast. Have a bite with us and then we'll go," Marie said.

"I'll go after a horse for Christine," Evelyn said. "Would you like to ride Pal or would you rather ride Headlight?"

"I'd like to ride Pal, Evelyn."

"Do you want to ride horseback too, Nonnie?" Marie asked. "Or do you want to ride in the wagon with me? Evelyn can bring in Headlight for you."

"I want to ride with you, Marie. We can have a good visit."

"I'm glad. I get lonely for the company of other women out here."

They cleared the table and stacked the dishes. Marie packed up some more food. Then they put the food and some blankets and the precious "piddow" in the wagon. Marie and Nonnie set off first, Jackie safely wedged between them.

Evelyn returned with Pal and saddled him. Then the four girls trotted off together.

"We've been wondering if you could come to Cheyenne for Frontier Days," Christine said. "Maybe you could bring a horse for me to ride. Then we can go in free."

"Probably some of us could come," Evelyn replied. "We can't all leave the homestead at once. The chores have to be done, you know."

"I hope I can go," Pearl said.

"I want to go too," Arlynn hastened to say.

"We'll have to talk to Marie about this," Pearl said. "Maybe none of us can go. It's a long ride."

As they approached the hills, Pearl noticed how the landscape began to change. The trees and bushes on the hills that looked tiny from a distance slowly grew larger. The rounded hills looked remarkably alike. They were called hogbacks. Some imaginative person had noticed that they resembled a row of gigantic hogs lying head to tail. The red ridges along the summits of the hogbacks, where erosion had washed away the soil, now could be seen as composed of jumbles of broken boulders.

They reached the hills and had to follow a tortuous route through a canyon between two hogbacks. Red rocks with pine trees and bushes growing in their fissures were on both sides of them.

When they got beyond what appeared from the

plain to be a single row of rounded hills, there were hills and more hills, meadows and more meadows.

"How far do these hills extend, Evelyn?" Pearl asked.

"I don't know. I'm not sure that anyone has gone all the way through them to find out. Mother says that they are part of the foothills of the Rocky Mountains so maybe they don't really end. They might just lead right into the mountains. I'd like to find out. Maybe someday I will."

"Evelyn, you'd get lost and starve to death," Pearl said. "Don't even think about it."

"I think I could live on fish and game."

"Well, don't ever try it. The mountains probably go on for hundreds of miles."

Evelyn was daring. You never knew what she would do.

The girls rode here and there to explore. They followed a mountain stream for some distance. Pearl loved the music of the waters as they swirled about between the boulders. They dismounted to get a drink. Cowboys rinse out their hats and use them for drinking vessels. The girls did this too. Their horses waded into the stream and drew up the water slowly and smoothly, with very little sound.

The girls stayed to pick up some of the most colorful pebbles in the sparkling water. When they remounted and trotted off they startled a bald eagle which took flight with a noisy flapping of its wings. Its great wingspread astounded them.

Later they stopped again for a drink of the ice-cold clear water. This water had its source in melting snow in the distant mountains. They were following the water course because it afforded the best route into the hills and would ensure their not getting lost.

At this stop Evelyn saw a water snake, caught it and began chasing Pearl with it. "I'm going to put it around your neck, Pearl!"

Pearl knew these snakes were harmless, but she did not want it to be draped around her neck. She had never even touched a snake. She began to run as fast as she could. She did not know she could move so fast. Running made her more panicky. She knew later that she should have stood her ground and pretended she was not scared. She should have taken the snake and turned it loose. But she was too scared. Eventually her niece gave up and put the snake down. She just liked to tease Pearl because she was a "tenderfoot," as anyone very far east of Wyoming was called.

Arlynn and Christine had watched this episode somewhat nervously, afraid that Evelyn might give up on Pearl and go after them.

The girls decided that they had better wait for the wagon to catch up with them. They had passed several places where there was a lot of dry wood lying about. They sat down and rested.

When Marie and Nonnie drove up, Pearl, Evelyn and Arlynn, and Christine at once besieged them with questions about Frontier Days.

"We have already discussed that. I have made a decision. Evelyn and Pearl can ride in and take a horse for Christine. Since Arlynn is younger she will have several chances to go. She can go next year."

Arlynn tried to get her mother to change her mind, but she knew someone had to stay home.

"We'll go on a little farther and find a good place to load the wagon with wood," Marie said. "Stay with us now. Don't go wandering off."

They finally stopped at a spot where there was plenty of wood. Everyone set to work, picking up gnarled limbs. These would be sawed into usable lengths when they were needed. The wagon was soon filled.

"We'll go a little farther for our picnic," Marie said. "I remember a fine grassy meadow near here."

Marie found the spot and she and Nonnie spread the blankets on the ground and began unpacking the lunch. Evelyn and Pearl built a small fire and started the coffee.

This was a place of great natural beauty. There were lovely wild flowers, including scarlet Indian paintbrush, Pearl's favorite. There was a grove of graceful quaking aspen trees. These trees have slender white trunks. Their small leaves made a delicate fluttering sound like the wings of many tiny birds.

"Pearl, in the fall these leaves turn golden," Marie said. "They are lovely now but I wish you could see them dressed in gold."

"I wish I could too, Marie. I've seen paintings of them but I know they would be even lovelier in reality."

They ate their delicious lunch. At the edge of the meadow the hills rose sharply and culminated in a striking red rock formation, broken into rough crags that formed interesting silhouettes against the sky. This feature was well enough known in the vicinity to be named Ragged Top. While they were munching on their chicken dinner, Marie silently pointed to a bobcat gazing at them from a rocky pinnacle. It was a beautiful animal, about twice the size of a big house cat. Its fur was grayish, streaked and spotted with black. Tufts of fur fluffed out from its ears. The bobcat regarded them curiously, unafraid, and then vanished. As it turned, they could see the short stumpy tail which gives it its name.

"It is wonderful to see wild animals and birds in their natural surroundings," Marie said. "A sight like this stays in my mind, bringing delight each time it is recalled."

They rested after eating and returned home happy. They had a good load of wood. They had had a change of scenery. More important, they had enjoyed a day with good friends.

Pearl wondered how there could be such a lovely place, with such varied and completely different landforms and vegetation, so close to the flat arid plains. What ancient upheaval had tossed up these rocky hills and hogbacks from deep in the earth? Where was the source of the crystal-clear waters which tumbled over and swished around the rocks?

12. The Quarry

Bill Eklund, one of the young men who worked at the limestone quarry in the hills, stopped in one evening for a visit. When he was about to leave he said, "Would you like to visit the quarry and learn about the work there?"

"I would," Evelyn said.

"I would," Jackie echoed.

Everyone was interested.

"Can you come next Monday? I'll talk to the boss and get permission to conduct a tour for you. Try to arrive by 1:30 Monday. If the boss doesn't agree, I'll come back and let you know. Otherwise, you'll understand that it's okay."

"We can be there by 1:30," Marie said. "That's a good time for us, because we can eat lunch early, ride to the quarry, and be back in time for chores."

On Monday they set off in time to reach the quarry by 1:30. When they arrived, Bill and Russell Melton were waiting for them. They showed them all around and explained the work. They answered numerous questions. Then Bill said, "Now we'll go down into a mine shaft where we get some of the limestone." He and Rusty had flashlights and led the way. It was spooky to be underground. Pearl feared that the mine shaft might collapse.

"It's nice and cool here," Evelyn said.

"We use dynamite to blast out the rock," Bill explained. "First a hole is drilled; then the dynamite is put into the hole and connected to a fuse. Everyone gets out and then the dynamite is exploded."

They continued farther into the shaft. Suddenly Bill said, "Stop where you are. We're going to turn off the flashlights and show you what real darkness is. Don't move!" Marie took Jackie's hand. "Okay. Now!" They were in total darkness. They could not see each other. They could not see the mine shaft.

"Turn on the flashlights," Jackie cried. "I don't like this."

The girls were giggling nervously to cover up their uneasiness. The flashlights beamed again. "When we speak of darkness we don't mean this kind," Marie said. "Usually we can see something dimly."

Pearl said, "Marie, do you remember the night last summer we rode back from a visit to a homesteader and we couldn't see anything?"

"That's right. We couldn't see our own horses; we couldn't see each other, and we had no idea of how to reach the places where the gates were or what direction to take to get home. We just sat on their backs, and they found the way. There was some light, enough for the horses to see, but not enough for us."

"We were very glad to see the light shining from the windows of the shack," Pearl remembered. "It was a long ride. I kept wondering if the horses really knew where they were going. I was afraid they'd plunge into a draw."

"Horses' eyes are better than ours," Marie said. "They can see when we can't."

"Like cats?" Evelyn asked.

"Yes, something like cats."

They began their walk back toward the entrance to the shaft. When they reached it, the sun was blinding after the dim light of the flashlights.

Bill said, "Rusty and I were talking about taking you to Cheyenne for dinner and a movie. You have been so good to welcome us to your home. Would you like to go?"

"Oh, yes!"

"That would be fun."

"When can we go?"

"Ruth will be here this weekend," Bill said. "I write to her now and then, and she said she'd be here. I want her to go too. So let's go Saturday."

Marie said, "I think Jackie and I will stay home. He would get too tired, and he wouldn't enjoy a movie. They're not for small children. You and I will do something that's fun, Jackie."

They rode home and discussed what they would wear. This occasion called for dresses. They would press their best dresses and be ready when Saturday came.

Ruth came Friday in her Chevy coupe. Pearl was delighted to see her. Now she had two of her sisters with her.

Bill and Rusty drove in Saturday in time to help with the chores, so they started to Cheyenne about 6:00. Ruth rode in the front seat between Bill and Rusty, and the three girls rode in back.

They had dinner at the Frontier Hotel. The three young girls were excited to be in such a fine restaurant. They felt grown up but shy and a little uneasy. However, in time they relaxed and had a good time.

The movie was entertaining. Pearl went to many movies at home, and had gone to her first "talkie," *The Jazz Singer*, the year before. Evelyn and Arlynn saw their first talkie that night.

It was late when they started home. The girls were tired and remembered they had to get up early to do the chores. They dozed off. The sound of rain hitting the top of the car awakened them. The wind was blowing hard. The rain intensified and flowed down the windshield in sheets. Bill could hardly see the road. He drove very slowly. The road became slick, and the car slipped off the roadway. Fortunately there was no ditch, but when he tried to drive back onto the road the car dug deeper and deeper into the mud puddles the wheels had churned up. He could not get back onto the road. He and Russell took off their shoes and pushed the car back onto the road while Ruth steered it. Bill and Rusty were soaking wet, so they took the car robe and wrapped it around Ruth to keep her dry. They continued on slowly. The rain finally stopped, but the road was still slick. The car slid off the road again about half an hour later. Bill and Rusty pushed it back. They kept their good humor in spite of everything.

After they passed the Inness ranch, a tire went flat. They had no spare tire. They jacked up the car and removed the tire. They got out a vulcanizing kit and repaired the inner tube, put it inside the tire and put the tire back on the wheel. Then they filled it full of air with a hand pump.

They finally reached the homestead at about three o'clock in the morning. Marie awoke and was surprised at how late it was. "I'm glad I was so sound asleep. I would have been very worried if I had known you still were not home at this hour. What happened?"

Bill told her about the problems with the car.

"Maybe horses are less trouble," Marie said.

"But you can't ride one to Cheyenne for dinner and a movie," Evelyn said. "We had a good time."

"Probably you had a better time than Bill and Rusty did," Marie commented.

Bill protested, "No, we enjoyed the evening."

"Maybe not the skidding and the mud and the flat tire, but the dinner and show were good," Rusty added.

Marie kindled a fire and made some coffee. Bill and

Rusty stood by the range trying to dry off. Marie set out some food and everyone had something to eat.

"I'm glad we don't have to work tomorrow," Rusty said.

After a short time, Rusty and Bill left, and Marie and Ruth and the girls hurried to get to bed for a few hours of sleep.

13. Ruth and Betty

After the chores were done in the morning the girls awakened Ruth. At breakfast they asked her many questions about college. They thought it must be very glamorous.

"Do you go to dances and parties, Ruth?" Pearl asked.

"Yes. I have a lot of fun. But college isn't all fun. I want to get good grades so I study hard. Marie, I've decided not to take that country school. I'm going to go to Colorado A&M in Fort Collins. I think I'll major in home economics – take the Smith-Hughes course. Then I can be a county extension agent. I'll never have any chance of advancement just teaching in country schools."

"I'm glad, Ruth. You have some college credits, and you should go on and finish. I'll miss having you near me though."

"I'll come to see you in the summer. Mother is enthusiastic about my doing this."

"Ruth," Pearl said, "tell me about the country school at the Kirkbrides' ranch, where you and Betty each taught one year. When Betty came home at Christmas time last year she burst into tears and said, "Baaa, Baaa!" She said that in the winter when the sheep were in the pens close to the house, she heard that baaing all day. It nearly drove her mad. The Kirkbrides ate mutton stew three times a day. She said one year of that was all she could take. Did you feel that way about it during your year there?"

"Well, I was more used to Wyoming. And I had

taught a country school for a year before that. Betty had never even been in a country school, so it was probably harder for her to adjust."

"Betty said she knew she was a big shock to the Kirkbrides," Pearl said. "She was a collegiate flapper with bobbed hair. She wore short dresses with a waistline at the hips. The Kirkbride women had long hair, dressed in old-fashioned clothes and wore long black stockings. She had her Victrola with her and played *Rhapsody in Blue* and *Nutcracker Suite*. They weren't used to any music other than hymns, and they thought this music was 'crazy.'" Everyone laughed.

"It was a hard experience for her," Ruth said. "But she needed money for college and she was lucky to get the school. A country school is the only kind you can get before you finish college."

"Did you have the same pupils as Betty when you taught there, Ruth?" Pearl asked. "She had five. Alexander and Elsie Kirkbride in eighth grade, Virginia Bevan in fifth, Junior Creathbaum in second, and his brother, Bobby, in first."

"I had the same pupils except the first grader. Alexander was my only eighth grader. His parents decided to have him repeat eighth grade so he and Elsie could start high school in Cheyenne together."

"Betty wrote us that you had the school so well organized that the pupils could tell her what to do. She said there were never any discipline problems. Mother had told her that country school children are very self-reliant. She did have a terrible experience though, with a Wyoming blizzard."

"What happened, Pearl?" Evelyn inquired. "Betty didn't get to visit us at all last winter. She was here before she started teaching. She had to study Wyoming history and something else in summer school at Laramie. Then she went right to the Kirkbride ranch."

"Betty didn't know how awful Wyoming blizzards could be," Pearl said. "It began to snow pretty hard one afternoon, and she sent the pupils home early. She stayed behind awhile to finish some work. It snowed harder, and the wind grew worse.

"When she started home she couldn't see anything so she followed a fence to the ranch. When she got there Elsie and Virginia weren't home yet. Mr. Kirkbride and his two older sons set out to look for them. Betty was frantic. She took up vigil first at one window and then at another. Once she thought she saw the girls far off on the plains, and she put on her wraps and went toward the spot. They weren't there. About six o'clock they found the girls at the Warren ranch. Nobody was home there, but the girls had gone in and waited there, cold and frightened. There was no wood in the wood box so they could not build a fire. They said they were playing in the snow and got lost. They tied themselves together with their scarves and stumbled on."

"The Kirkbrides should have told Betty what to do in case of storms," Ruth said. "She should have kept the children at the school or have gone home with them to see that they stayed by the fence."

"Betty said it was not snowing too hard when she sent the children home," Pearl said. "Elsie and Virginia should have stayed with Alexander and the others. They were being silly and playing. Even the little children got home safely."

Pearl added, "Betty wrote that she has a job working for her room and board next year. Professor and Mrs. Littell have four children and a new baby is expected. She can stay with them during her junior and senior years and help with the work."

"I will have to find work, too," Ruth said.

"Edna really started something by going to college, didn't she?" Marie said. "Of course Earl was the first to go on to college." Everyone fell silent thinking of the brother they had lost.

Ruth broke the silence. "You started something by coming to Wyoming too, Marie. Phebe came out here and met the man she married. Then Betty and I came to teach country school. Edna has been here once, and Pearl has been here several summers. Wyoming seems to attract us like a magnet."

"I love Wyoming!" Pearl added. "I want to live here when I finish college."

14. The Pack-Saddle Camping Trip

After another week or so of working with the ponies Pearl wanted a change. One day she said to Evelyn, "Let's ride up into the breaks to camp overnight or maybe two nights."

"Good idea," Evelyn said. "We'll camp near that old Indian camping ground."

"We should make a list of what we need to take with us," Pearl said. "One thing is plenty of bedding. And a tarpaulin to cover our bed in case of rain. What food shall we take?"

"Bread, butter, eggs, potatoes, coffee, milk and stuff to make pancakes with. And some things from the garden."

"We have to take a frying pan and some lard. And something to boil coffee in."

"We can take the 45 revolver and shoot a rabbit for meat. A rifle would be too big to take."

"Don't forget matches to start the fire. And let's take a kerosene lantern. And the books we are reading." Pearl was a bookworm and had brought many books in her trunk.

"We'll need hobbles for our horses so they won't run away," Evelyn said. "I'll ride Waltina."

"I'll ride Pal."

"Let's take Dirk along," Evelyn suggested. "A dog will make us feel safer. And we'll take a leash so we can fasten it around a wrist at night. Otherwise, he'll go home when we're asleep."

"Our horses can't carry all that stuff. We'll have to

take a pack horse."

"We'll take Tiny as a pack horse."

They made a list that grew longer and longer. They thought of peanut butter, salt and pepper, jackets, a deck of cards.

When they asked Marie, she said they could go. She could manage the chores. Pearl and Evelyn planned to have the others bring a picnic and join them the second evening of their camping trip. They knew a good place for a picnic in a ravine, out of the wind. They told Marie where it was.

That evening a few of the young men from the limestone quarry stopped in to visit. The girls decided to invite them too. They could bring Marie, Arlynn, and Jackie up to the breaks in their cars. They would all have a picnic, build a bonfire, sing songs and tell stories.

The girls gathered everything together that night and, in the morning after chores, they made three bundles and tied two small ones on the backs of their saddles and a larger one on Tiny. They set out, with Dirk joyously circling about and dashing after every cottontail and jackrabbit that he saw. He never gave up, though the rabbits almost always escaped into their burrows. Pearl hoped he would not catch one today. She remembered the terrified cry of a rabbit he once caught. Until then she did not know they could make any sound.

They crossed the plain and then wound their way among the breaks. When they found the old Indian campground they unpacked and took off their ponies' saddles and bridles. They put the hobbles on the horses' front feet and the three animals moved away slowly, grazing contentedly. The hobbles were leather straps with buckles. They were connected by chains long enough so the horses could take short steps.

Next they gathered some good-sized stones and arranged them in a small circle. Their campfire would be kindled here. They did not use stones from the circles the Indians had made. They hoped those stones would always remain there. Enough dry greasewood and sagebrush branches were gathered to last throughout their stay.

"Evelyn, let's put our bedroll where one of the tepees stood." Pearl felt the presence of the vanished Indians. "Can't you imagine how the Indian women erected their tepees here? Then they would be busy taking care of their children, making clothes, and preparing food. They did almost all the work. The men did the hunting and made the arrowheads and bows and arrows. They had a good view of the prairie from the top of this hill. Maybe they would see a buffalo herd moving toward the wallow. Then they would ride down the draw and get close to them before dashing after them to kill a lot of them."

Evelyn said, "I don't think they would kill more than one at a time. This was a small encampment. One buffalo would provide a lot of meat. I've read that it was the white hunters who killed so many buffalo that they almost became extinct. They often took just the hides and left the meat to rot."

"That's right," Pearl said. "I have read a lot of stories about Indians. The boys took care of the horses so they wouldn't run away or be stolen."

They made their bed carefully. The large tarp was stretched out on the ground; the blankets and pillows were placed on it, and the extra canvas was folded over the top.

"Now we should take the milk, butter, eggs, fresh

vegetables and anything else we want to keep cold to the spring in the cave," Pearl suggested. They gathered things together and went to the spring.

"Pearl, we have to dig a basin to collect the water so it will be deep enough to cover these jars."

This task took a long time, because the only tools they had were some rough rocks. It was tiresome.

"I'm getting hungry," Evelyn said. "Why don't we eat our lunch here in the cave? Will you go back to get some bread and the peanut butter, some knives and the tin cups? I'll work on this while you are gone."

"All right. I'll bring some cookies and fudge too."

Pearl was beginning to realize that camping out was hard work. She missed Marie, Arlynn and Jackie and wondered what they were doing.

When she returned they made sandwiches and munched on crisp radishes and carrots. The cold milk was delicious. Candy and cookies were a satisfying dessert. Dirk was fed two sandwiches and a piece of fudge.

They washed their cups and put away the food.

"Let's go back to camp and rest a while," Pearl suggested. "We can read and play cards."

"Then we'll go exploring this afternoon," Evelyn said. "Let's ride all the way to the end of the Farthing ranch. I've never done that. I don't know how far it will be."

They played rummy and read. Evelyn read only books about the West. Pearl read every book she could get her hands on – all the way from trash to the classics. Sister Edna had suggested titles that she was reading in college: John Galsworthy's and George Eliot's and Thomas Hardy's novels. Pearl read them avidly even though there was much in them that she did not fully understand.

Finally Evelyn asked, "Shall we get our horses now and go?"

They took bridles and found Waltina and Pal. They decided to ride bareback. They proceeded at a trot, Dirk racing round and round them, until they reached the Farthing lands.

"Why don't we go down into the draw and ride in it as far as we can?" Pearl suggested.

The horses slid down the steep bank, and they rode along exploring the larger gullies leading into the draw. They noticed one which had an entrance too narrow for their horses.

"Pearl, let's explore this one on foot."

They tied the horses to sagebrush bushes and went into the recessed area. There was a spring near the entrance.

"Evelyn, I see something shiny over there where Dirk went." Dirk had disappeared into a cave-like place about two feet above the floor of the gully. Pearl started toward it, closely followed by Evelyn. "Look at this complicated metal thing. This part is copper tubing. Why in the world would anybody put a contraption like this out here in the middle of nowhere?"

"I think maybe it's a still, Pearl. I've seen pictures of them. So, someone's making whiskey out here. It's like the moonshiners in the southern hills."

"Yes," Pearl said. "Herbert's first job as a postal inspector was in the Kentucky hill country. He had to ride a mule to get to the little hill towns. He was warned that he must hire a guide from the particular region where he was working. Otherwise the natives who were making moonshine might mistake him for a 'revenooer' and take a potshot at him."

"I've heard that gangsters run the sale of bootleg liquor," Evelyn said. "They have shooting wars over it."

"That's in the big cities, I think, Evelyn. Do you suppose it's dangerous for us to find this and to be here?"

"Maybe; we won't tell anyone except Mother."

"It's been used recently, Evelyn. See how shiny and clean it is. Someone has carefully leveled the floor of this tiny cave. Let's get out of here."

"Why don't we take some sagebrush branches and drag them over the tracks we made here?"

They obliterated their tracks, but the brush marks showed plainly. They jumped onto their horses and hurried on their way.

Pearl was worried. "I hope we don't meet anyone in this draw."

As they rode along they heard a bull bellowing. Rounding a bend in the draw they saw the bull with a herd of cows. He was huge. He was tearing up a bank of earth with his horns and pawing the dirt. Another bull was answering his roars from a distance.

"Let's go topside," Pearl said. "I don't want to ride past him."

"Pearl, he won't charge us. He's just warning that other bull to stay away."

After they had scrambled up the steep side of the draw, Pearl said, "I've been thinking about the still. It's not very big. No one could distill enough whiskey with that to be in the bootlegging business. Maybe some cowhands are making it just for themselves."

"You're right. Let's not tell anyone. It's our secret. When we ride to Iron Mountain though let's remember to look over this way to see if there is any steam or smoke. Maybe we'll see someone riding over there."

"It's a lot of trouble to go to just to get some whiskey," Pearl said.

"They probably think it's sort of fun."

"I hear people talk about making bathtub gin in the city. I don't know anyone who does it though." Pearl looked around. "Let's turn back now and go to the camp. I don't think the Farthing ranch ever ends."

"How about riding on the road the rest of the way?" Evelyn said. "I'll race you!"

Waltina and Pal entered into the spirit of the race and did their best. An excited Dirk joined in.

When they reached the road they saw a dead cow lying near it. The stench was overpowering. The carcass was already bloated, the feet sticking up grotesquely. A coyote was slinking away. Dirk ran after him, barking furiously.

"Probably injured by a car or truck," Pearl said. "What a waste!"

"The coyotes will soon dispose of the carcass," Evelyn said. "They keep the prairie clean by eating carrion. Of course, they do attack lambs and calves too. But I can't imagine how horrible it would be without coyotes. There are so many animals here. There'll be only bones and hide left here in a few days. Many coyotes will be attracted."

Dirk returned and was sniffing around the carcass. The girls called him sharply and galloped away as fast as they could go. They saw some horses gathered near a water hole and stopped so Waltina and Pal could get a drink. Dirk lapped up water thirstily too.

When they got back to their camp they built a fire and boiled some coffee. Then they went to the cave for supplies. They cooked raw fried potatoes and eggs and ate more fresh vegetables. Cookies and milk were dessert. They read until it got dark, and then they lighted the lantern and continued to read.

"Let's not do the dishes. We can wash them in the morning. I don't want to go to the cave now," Pearl said.

"Tomorrow let's ride back into the breaks to explore. Maybe we can find another Indian campground."

"I want to do that. But now let's go to bed. I'm tired. I'm going to leave all my clothes on except my boots. It's really cold up here."

They settled down in bed. There was no moon, and they could not see anything beyond the feeble light of the dying campfire. It was a little scary – as though they were enclosed in a black box with tiny lights above. When the fire died out the stars were brighter. There were millions and billions of them, diamonds on black velvet. They saw many falling stars and decided that they would each watch one-half the sky for falling stars.

"Look, there's one!"

"Look over here. I see one too."

While the girls watched the falling stars make streaks of varying length in the sky they heard the weird howls and yelps of coyotes calling to each other. This was a familiar sound. They heard it every night. Somehow the sound was different and threatening there in the dark, this far from home.

Dirk, leashed so he would not go home, was curled up on Evelyn's side of the bedding. The girls finally fell asleep. Sometime in the night, she did not have any idea of the actual time, Pearl heard Dirk growl. She touched Evelyn on the shoulder and whispered, "Evelyn listen. Dirk sees or hears something out there. What do you suppose it is?"

Dirk was standing and pulling on the leash, staring into the darkness. His warning growls became louder.

"Maybe someone saw us ride up here – some bad people." Evelyn answered. "There aren't any dangerous animals up here."

"Maybe it's a coyote creeping close to us."

"Coyotes don't attack people," Evelyn said as she peered into the darkness. "I have the pistol here." The girls had both crawled out of the covers and were sitting up, trying to see what was out there where Dirk was looking.

All at once he moved back onto the blankets and began to turn about in circles as dogs do when they are ready to go to sleep.

"We're silly," said Evelyn. "Probably he saw a rabbit. You know how they run and play at night." The girls both giggled and settled down as though to sleep. But Pearl was still listening and trying to see into the inky darkness.

Finally they went to sleep, only to be awakened in the middle of the night by a sudden, drenching rainstorm. It does not rain very often in Wyoming, but it poured down that night. The water seeped in under the tarp. They tried to arrange some dry parts of the blankets under the tarpaulin, but there did not seem to be any dry parts. Then they decided to put the tarp over their heads like a makeshift tent. Dirk was between them, his wet fur odorous. The tarp was old and soon soaked through. The rain stopped finally, but they were miserably cold and wet. They huddled in the wet blanket and tarp to keep out of the wind. Wet blankets wrapped closely about them were better than nothing.

They waited anxiously for the first glimmer of dawn. When they could see, they got up and hurried to make a fire. The wood was wet. It would not ignite. "Let's pour all the kerosene from the lantern onto the wood," Evelyn said. That started the fire. They were ravenously hungry.

"Let's go after a rabbit," Evelyn suggested.

"I'll stay here and mix pancake batter and get things ready for breakfast. I'll get the things from the spring, too."

"You never want to go hunting," Evelyn said accusingly, "but you like to eat rabbit meat."

Pearl recognized the contradiction in this, but she did not like to see anything killed. It was especially nightmarish to her when chickens were killed and their headless bodies went flopping all over the ground.

"There's only one gun, Evelyn."

"Okay. I will be back soon."

Evelyn returned within half an hour with a rabbit already skinned and gutted. They had a delicious breakfast of pancakes, fried rabbit and coffee. Dirk had all the pancakes and rabbit he could eat. Then they took their dishes to the cave and washed them and stored the cold things again.

A beautiful sunrise was followed by an increasingly hot sun. The sun and the ever-present wind soon dried the ground and partially dried their clothes. They spread the blankets and tarp out to dry.

Then they went to locate their horses so they could go exploring. But they could not find them.

"Maybe they're over that hill," Evelyn said. "I'll go that way, and you go in the other direction."

The horses were not in either place. All three were

gone. The girls were dismayed. They could not go exploring. They would have to walk home. It was not really far down to the homestead – about three-fourths of a mile. But they had a lot of things to carry.

"They must have walked all night instead of grazing," Evelyn said. "Or maybe they rocked back and forth 'til they worked up to a gallop. Some horses learn to do that with hobbles on."

"We can't carry these things all the way home," Pearl grumbled. "How will it look for us to plod home carrying heavy loads when we rode here expecting to stay at least two days?"

"We will leave most of the things here. Maybe we can catch the horses on the way home."

They turned Dirk loose, and he ran home as fast as he could go. They trudged along carrying a few things in bundles on their backs. They did not see any horses. They would have to face the humiliation of walking in.

They knew the folks at home would be waiting to make fun of them for this inglorious ending of their adventure. Sure enough, they could see Marie, Arlynn and Jackie coming out of the house to watch their slow progress. They had time to make up a mocking jingle:

> Here come the campers
> A bundle on each back.
> Where are the horses
> That they seem to lack?
> Was the night delightful,
> Snug and warm and dry?
> Or was it simply frightful?
> Did you want to cry?

Looking at the laughing faces and hearing the derisive verse composed in their honor amused the girls, and they burst into laughter too. They were glad to be home even though they were ridiculed.

They rode up and brought their things home that afternoon. The next night they had a picnic in the breaks as they had planned. Their friends from the quarry drove them there in their cars.

Marie set out the picnic while the others gathered wood for a big fire. They sat around the fire eating and talking. They sang all the songs they could think of and told stories. It was a beautiful starry night. Not a drop of rain fell that night or for several weeks afterwards.

15. Goodbye to Snowball and Midnight

One day Mr. Farthing drove up in a stock truck. Another man was with him. Pearl and Evelyn were working with some ponies in the corral. The men walked over to watch them.

"How is it going with the ponies?" Mr. Farthing said. "Do you have any trained yet? This is Mr. Harris from Cheyenne. He wants to buy two tame ponies for his grandchildren."

Their hearts sank. They would lose two of their dear little ponies. They knew this would happen some day. They would lose all of them except Merrilegs. It seemed too soon though. They had hoped to keep them all until the end of summer.

"We have two gentled besides the one we broke for Arlynn," Evelyn said. "There is a beautiful one that's mostly white with some pretty tan markings. We call her Snowball. And there's a tiny one, coal black, named Midnight. We'll go get them for you."

"They've started training these others too, Mr. Farthing," Marie said. She had come to the corral to talk to Mr. Farthing. She invited the men in for coffee while Evelyn and Pearl brought in Snowball and Midnight.

When they were in the corral, the men came out to see them. Mr. Farthing was pleased to see how tame and how well-trained Snowball and Midnight were. He praised Evelyn and Pearl for the good job they had done. "They are both much tamer than I expected."

"We love them and we have spent a lot of time with them," Pearl said. "Jackie and Arlynn ride them too."

"I want them both," Mr. Harris said. "The large one will be just right for my nine-year-old granddaughter, and the little one will be the right size for her five-year-old brother."

"I want to buy Midnight." Jackie said. "I have some money in my piggy bank. I don't want him to go away."

"You have a pony, Jackie," Marie said. "When you are too big for Blackie you can have your own horse. You would like a big horse, wouldn't you?"

"Yes, I want one now. But let me ride Midnight just one more time."

Mr. Harris put Jackie on the little pony and was pleased to see how well it was trained, turning and stopping at Jackie's signals. Jackie got off and patted Midnight's velvety nose. He said, "Goodbye, Midnight. Be a good pony."

Then he went to Snowball and said a fond farewell to him. Snowball was a very gentle pony.

"My granddaughter and grandson will love these ponies," Mr. Harris said. "We'll take good care of them."

They put a ramp down from the back of the stock truck. Evelyn and Pearl led the ponies up it and tied them. Then the men drove off, leaving five sad people.

Marie remarked, "I like Mr. Harris, and I am sure he will see that Snowball and Midnight are well cared for."

"I hope the children love them as much as we do," Pearl said.

"I'm sure they will," Marie assured her.

Pearl

Marie's homestead

Jack Achttien

Marie and Jack's horse, Smoky

The store at Iron Mountain

Pearl and Orphan

Pearl, Christine Dunn and Evelyn

Orphan, Jackie and Dirk

Evelyn and Tiny

Pearl and Smoky

Ruth and Headlight

Marie and a friend returning with wood

Edna's Model T

Edna, Evelyn and Pearl on Ragged Top

OFFICIAL PROGRAM

1897 CHEYENNE FRONTIER DAYS 1928

"THE DADDY OF 'EM ALL"

1928 FRONTIER DAYS COMMITTEE

WILLIAM G. "BILL" HAAS, Chairman
EDW. T. STOREY, Treasurer
ROBT. D. HANESWORTH, Secretary

R. J. HOFMANN, Tickets
JAMES BUCHANAN, Indians
GEORGE F. JONES, Music-Parades

Arena Directors:
Wm. G. "Bill" Haas, Cheyenne, Wyo.
Dan Clark, Cheyenne, Wyo.

Arena Judges:
George Marty, Horse Creek, Wyo.
Ray Bell, Brooklyn, N. Y.
Hugh Strickland, Hollywood, Calif.

Flag Judge: Ernest Greea, Hereford Ranch, Wyo.

Track Judges:
George M. Hiatt, Wheatland
Gregory Powell, Cheyenne, Wyo.
Fred Boice, Cheyenne, Wyo.

Official Timers:
Wm. F. DeVere, Cheyenne, Wyo.
Capt. R. G. Ayers, Ft. D. A. Russell, Wyo.
Geo. Goobs, Cheyenne, Wyo.

FIFTH DAY OF SHOW JULY 28th, 1928

Event No. 1—Grand Opening Entry and Parade of Contestants.

Event No. 2—On Track. Calf Riding for boys under 16 years of age.
Christine Dunn, Pearl Rumble, Arlyan Rumble, Blase Sanchez, Jack Murray, Joe Simon, Mike Connor, Vernon Jones, Harry Lewis, Billie Brimmer.

Christine, Pearl and Arlynn in the Calf Riding event (underlined)

Homestead on the Range ~ 99

Marie and her daughters: Ruth, Phebe, Marie, Betty, Pearl, Edna

16. Billy Goat

Marie drove the cart to the store one day. She took Jackie with her, and they took a side trip to visit a homesteader.

This homesteader had a herd of goats. They were all over the place baaing to each other and standing on the roofs of sheds, climbing into wagon beds and climbing through corral poles. Jackie was fascinated. He had never seen goats before. The family offered to give him a tiny kid. It was only a few weeks old. It had two little knobs on its head, the beginnings of the horns it would have later.

Marie thanked the man, and when they left Jackie was holding his new little pet.

At the homestead Billy was happy following Jackie about. Jackie fed him from a bottle at first, but Billy was always adept at getting at the chickens' feed, grain, sour skim milk, and water. The girls were kept busy refilling them.

Billy could get through any fence. He took to going into the draw and getting into the precious garden there. The barbed wire fence that kept out the cattle and horses was no barrier to him. The family depended upon the garden produce for all their vegetables. The stores at Iron Mountain and Horse Creek did not carry much fresh produce. All the locals grew their own vegetables. So they had to watch Billy constantly and go down and drag him out of the garden and up the hill.

Like any goat Billy loved to butt his head against things. Jackie would get down on all fours and play butting games with him. This worried Marie, although the impact did not seem too great because the goat was tiny. It did not worry Jackie.

Sometimes Billy would surprise one of the others by attacking from behind. If they happened to be leaning over they could lose their balance. They laughed at these pranks but noticed that Billy was growing fast and wondered if it would be so funny when he weighed more and had real horns.

Billy loved to climb onto the roof of the chicken house and shed. They figured that his sharp hooves could damage the roofs.

They could not keep him in a corral. He could wriggle through the poles. They did not want to tie him up; it would be cruel, because he needed to romp around as all young animals need to do. Jackie was too young to be given the full responsibility of watching him. He would become engrossed in playing and not notice that Billy had strayed away.

On wash days they had to be especially careful. Clothes dry very quickly in the dry winds of Wyoming. But unless everyone maintained constant surveillance until the clothes dried, and snatched them off the line and whisked them to safety inside the house, they would discover Billy munching contentedly on a sleeve or chewing a corner off a sheet.

Marie knew he had to go. But how to separate Jackie from his pet? There was never a boy who loved animals more than he did. He could not bear to have anyone mistreat any living creature.

His mother figured out how to persuade him to give up Billy. She appealed to his love of animals. She said, "Jackie, do you remember the herd of goats at the homestead? They were having so much fun. Billy has been very happy with you, but now that he is growing up he will be unhappy without other goats. He'll want to mate with a female goat."

"Can't we get some more goats and bring them here for company for him?"

"No, Jackie. We don't have enough pasture for a herd of goats and our horses and cattle. And he is getting into the garden every day. It's best for him to go back to the goat herd."

Jackie was finally persuaded. "Can I go there to see him sometimes?"

"Of course. You'll be surprised to see how big he'll be. He will be happier there, Jackie."

The girls knew they would be happier. Billy kept them too busy. Besides they would not have to keep looking nervously behind them every time they stepped out into the yard.

So Marie and Jackie took Billy home. Jackie saw him rejoin all the goats there. He felt good about sacrificing his own wishes to make Billy happy.

17. Runaway

"I need flour and sugar and chicken feed," Marie announced one evening. "I'm going to take the two-wheeled cart and drive to Iron Mountain tomorrow."

"Can I go too?" was the chorus that immediately followed.

"Of course. You can all go. Jackie can ride in the cart with me. One of you girls can ride in the cart too."

"I'll ride Waltina," Evelyn said.

"I'll ride Tiny," Pearl said.

"I'll ride Blackie," Arlynn said.

Marie had everything planned. "We'll get up half an hour early, and one of you can bring in the horses; the others can follow with the cows. By the time the cows are here we can have the team hitched and the riding horses saddled. We'll have time to feed the chickens and pigs. When the cows get in we will milk and do the milk chores. We'll be at Iron Mountain soon after the store opens."

"Can I get some candy?" Jackie asked.

"Yes, you can all buy some."

"We'll get our mail too," Pearl said. "Probably Mother has written."

In the morning when Pearl and Evelyn tried to catch their horses, they had problems. Waltina came up to the pan of oats that Evelyn swished about enticingly, but when Evelyn tried to put a rein over Waltina's neck she whirled about and ran away. Tiny was skittish too. So Evelyn tried Baldy and succeeded.

"Pearl, you drive the horses in. I'll find the cows

and bring them in on foot."

"No, Evelyn, you get up behind me and first we'll ride to find the cows. Then we'll draw straws to see who walks the cows in." Pearl drew the short straw and started the cows on their slow trek home.

Everything went according to plan, and the group set off for Iron Mountain. The three riders were soon far ahead, although Marie was traveling fast in the cart. It was much more comfortable than the spring wagon, and the horses could pull it easily.

When the girls reached the store they tied their horses to the hitching post and went inside to visit with Tom and Irene. Pearl asked about mail, and there were two letters, one from her mother and one from Edna. Both were addressed to Marie, so the girls had to wait until she arrived.

They caught up on the latest news about people living near Iron Mountain. In this sparsely-settled country "near" could mean within fifty or one hundred miles. They had some news to relay about people from around Horse Creek too. People took time to stop and visit. They were never too busy. Human contacts were precious.

They were all watching the road for Marie and Jackie as they talked. When the cart arrived they went outside to greet them and tie up the team. Marie visited with Tom and Irene, and they handed her the letters. She read them aloud.

There was exciting news from Edna. She was driving the old Model T Ford that she had just bought to Yellowstone Park in August. A friend from Prophetstown, Illinois, where Edna was teaching was coming too. And a Mrs. Warman from Cheyenne would go with them to Yellowstone. Ruth was coming from Laramie to join them.

Pearl made up her mind that she would wheedle

Edna into taking her along. There would be room for five people in the car. She wanted to see Old Faithful Geyser, the bubbling hot springs, and Yellowstone Falls and canyon. Especially she wanted to see the grizzly bears.

Her mother's letter told news from home and announced that she was planning to come to Wyoming in time for Frontier Days.

When they had chosen the candy and gum they wanted, and Tom had loaded the one hundred pound sacks of sugar and flour and chicken feed into the cart, Pearl asked if she could drive the team home. Jackie seized upon this opportunity to beg Marie to let him ride home on a pony. Eventually Marie agreed. Jackie rode little Blackie and Arlynn rode Tiny. Jackie was an excellent rider; he had begun riding almost as soon as he had learned to walk.

Pearl had a plan. She wanted to enlist Marie in a campaign to get Edna to take her to Yellowstone. She knew it would not be difficult. Marie always wanted people to enjoy themselves. She readily promised to help Pearl.

As they jogged along, they talked of many things. Marie knew all the lore of the country, and her stories fascinated Pearl.

All at once a jackrabbit bounded across the road almost under the feet of the horses. Dolly and Babe snorted and took off at a wild gallop. Pearl pulled firmly on the reins and spoke soothingly to them, but they would not stop. Marie wanted to leave Pearl in charge but finally took the reins. When she failed to bring the team to walk, she shouted, "Hang on tight!" and slackened the reins. She took the long ends of the reins in hand and gave first Babe and then Dolly a smart slap on the rump. The cart careened down the road, the flour, sugar, and feed sacks shifting about in the back of the cart.

"Are you scared, Pearl?"

"Not with you driving!"

When the team grew tired and wanted to slow down Marie urged them on. They caught up with the surprised riders who realized what was happening and held their horses back. Finally Babe and Dolly could not continue and slowed to a walk. Their necks and flanks were covered with foam, and they were breathing noisily.

Marie said, "Horses are stronger than a person. You have to use your wits to control them. This will be a lesson to Dolly and Babe. They will not be anxious to run away for a while."

Later, this advice was a help to everyone. If a pony ran away with them, they just urged it to run faster. It learned they were not afraid and learned that this tactic did not get rid of a rider.

Evelyn, Arlynn, and Jackie caught up with the cart. Marie said, "Jackie, are you getting tired of riding?"

Jackie answered, "I'm not tired. I want to ride Blackie all the way home."

This was the longest ride he had ever taken. They were all proud of his determination. He rode off, sitting easily on fat little Blackie, who was taking two steps to every step the other horses were taking. Every now and then Blackie nipped at Waltina and Tiny as they passed him. He wanted to be out in front.

18. Whang

"Let's start training Whang today," Evelyn suggested. They had been putting off working with this pony, because he was so wild-eyed and rambunctious.

Whang was a beautiful pony. Marie named him. He was a large pinto gelding. His colored spots were the palest tan, really a sort of yellowish white. Whang is one name for rawhide, which is the same color. Somehow the name also suggested the liveliness of the pony.

Pearl and Evelyn had become quite skilled in dropping the loop of the lariat over the ponies' heads. It was fairly easy, because the ponies usually circled the corral. Whang was the exception. He watched that rope and dodged and whirled about. The rope dropped uselessly onto his back and fell off. Eventually they got it around his neck. He went crazy. He reared and plunged and pulled away from them. The girls both pulled on the rope and looped it around the snubbing post. When they forced him toward it, he suddenly ceased resistance, reared, and came at them on his hind legs, striking out with his hooves. They managed to avoid him, but they were scared.

A convertible driven by a young woman came up to the corral in a cloud of dust. The woman got out of the car, strode over to the gate, opened it, and joined them. They recognized her as the older daughter of a rancher who lived a long way from them.

She had a quirt in her hand. "Let me show you how to handle this animal!" she yelled. She pulled him closer to the post, got a short hold on the rope around his neck, and began hitting him with the quirt. The quirt was a flexible short whip of woven rawhide with buckshot inside. The blows from a quirt are painful.

"I'll teach you to behave!" She continued striking him.

"Please don't hit him," Pearl begged. "He's a wild pony. He doesn't know any better."

Marie was working in the house. She heard the commotion and hurried over to the corral. "Please come with me to the house," she said to the woman. "The girls must train the ponies. This is the first session with this pony. They want to teach him to trust people so he'll be safe for children. Let's go have a cup of coffee and some cake and have a good visit."

Marie did not want to offend the visitor. The woman's family was highly respected in the country. They had been good to the family. Ruth had taught eighth grade studies to their youngest daughter one year; she was the only pupil in the school district. Ruth boarded and roomed with them. Since it seemed ridiculous to travel each day to a tiny schoolhouse located out in the middle of nowhere, the family suggested holding classes in the ranch house. So a room was outfitted there with a blackboard, globe, anything Ruth needed.

Marie explained to the visitor about the girls' big summer project. After a good visit she left.

Evelyn and Pearl sacked Whang until he stood still when the sack was tossed onto him, then put a halter on him and tried to teach him to lead. He reared and struck at them. They had to give him a lot of rope to avoid his hooves.

On succeeding days they tried until finally they could lead him. Then they saddled him so he would become accustomed to carrying something on his back. He tried in every way to buck off the saddle but could not. They continued this until he accepted the saddle peacefully.

They got him used to a bridle and led him about with bridle and saddle on him.

Next they had to ride him. Bareback. They were afraid of what he might do. It was Pearl's turn to take the first ride. She knew what was going to happen. She got on; Whang was turned loose and ran into the side of the corral, hurting her leg. Then he bucked and promptly threw her off. Evelyn was supposed to get on next, but she did not want to. Pearl was angry, because this was their agreement. But Marie took Evelyn's side. She did not have to get on if she did not want to. Marie was right, of course. Pearl thought Evelyn was not afraid of anything. She found out Evelyn was as scared as she was.

Another day they tried again and finally were successful in staying on. So they thought they had taught him to trust and accept them.

One day when Pearl was riding him in the corral, he suddenly reared up so high that he fell over backward. This is feared more than anything, because the horse might fall on the rider. It would be fatal. Fortunately he fell to one side, and Pearl fell to the other side. Her ankle was sprained, and she had to be carried to the house. The sprain was painful but proved not too serious. After a few days she could walk on it. This was the only real injury the girls received while riding the wild ponies. They were very fortunate.

Eventually Whang was trained. He learned to trust people. He would always be a more spirited and unpredictable pony than the others. He would be fine for a ranch-bred boy or girl. The girls would tell Mr. Farthing to be sure to sell him to a confident, experienced rider.

19. Visit to Frenchy and Marguerite

"Pearl, let's ride up into the hills and visit Frenchy and Marguerite," Evelyn suggested one evening.

Marie commented, "That's a good idea. Marguerite must be very lonely living so far away from any woman."

"Yes, let's go," Evelyn said. "I like Marguerite and Frenchy. Let's start early in the morning. Can we take them some little present?"

"You could make some cookies tonight," Marie said.

Evelyn and Pearl made cookies and packed them carefully in a tin box so they would not get broken.

Marguerite and Frenchy were from Canada, young people in their twenties. Their homestead was far back in the hills. The girls were not sure that they would be home. They thought that they would be because they had livestock to care for.

The girls always enjoyed riding in the hills because of the varied scenery. As they rode along enjoying the beauty of the hills, they heard a well-known shrill buzzing sound. This was the buzzing warning that a rattlesnake gives when it feels threatened. It can be heard from many yards away and it does not sound like a rattle. It is too fast for that.

The ponies shied away from the snake which was coiled, with its head lifted and its tail shaking rapidly. They rode a few yards away, watching carefully for another snake.

Whenever ranchers or homesteaders saw a rattler they killed it if possible. The snakes were a threat to livestock and to people. Few snakes remained on the homestead. The first time Marie's parents visited the homestead her mother almost stepped on a rattler. She had gone for a walk and was just about to put her foot down on a snake when it rattled. She saw the snake and sprang back just in time.

The girls were wearing riding boots. Snakes were one reason for the boots. The leather afforded good protection from the sharp fangs that inject the poison. The snakes are not aggressive. They do not chase people. They just coil up and give a warning. The largest ones are about eight feet long. They can strike only about two-thirds of their length. The girls dismounted, and Pearl held the horses. Evelyn gathered some stones and killed the snake. It had a large bulge in its middle — a sign that it had eaten recently. Snakes swallow their prey whole. Their jaws are not fused together but are joined by cartilage that is elastic. They can swallow an animal much bigger around than they are. First they bite the victim, injecting poison from their fangs. Then they swallow it whole, head first. The meal is digested slowly. They do not have to eat very often.

These snakes were locally called diamondback rattlers, but they were really prairie rattlers. Rattlers are beautiful creatures. There is a showy black diamond pattern on their backs, and the background color is grey and dull gold. This was a big one with many rattles. Pearl thought it was a shame to kill it. It was not near any house. She had learned in science class that snakes are useful. They eat the small rodents which would multiply beyond belief without snakes and birds of prey and coyotes to eat them. She knew that ranchers killed snakes, coyotes, hawks and eagles, and even badgers. She wondered what the country would be like with all the wild things killed.

Evelyn decided to skin the snake and take the skin

and rattles home. It still moved though dead from a smashed head. Evelyn took out a pocket knife and made a cut down its underside. Then they saw that the snake had swallowed a gopher very recently. Its fur was intact; it had not been digested at all. The snake, once a beautiful creature, was now a grisly sight.

Evelyn carefully removed the snake's skin with rattles attached. Somehow the skin did not look as beautiful as when it was on a living creature. She draped it over the back of the saddle and tied it on with the saddle strings.

They rode on, stopping occasionally for a cold drink from a mountain stream. Eventually they reached their friends' little cabin. They had probably built it themselves. There was plenty of wood in the hills. The cabin was on a rise not far from the stream. The girls had ridden about six miles to get there.

They had a good visit with their friends and a refreshing lunch. Marguerite was pretty. She had dark curly hair and dark eyes. She was short and looked like a little girl. She was a pleasant, smiling woman. There did not seem to be much of an age gap between her and the girls, because she was so small. But she was a mature woman, and they were just kids.

When they told Marguerite and Frenchy about the snake and showed them the skin, Marguerite had a snake story to tell too.

"You remember our team of mares? They had fine colts in the early spring. One day all four were bitten on their noses by rattlesnakes while they were grazing," Marguerite related sadly. "The colts were dead when we discovered what had happened. Their heads were terribly swollen."

"I didn't know what to do to help the mares," Frenchy said. "Their heads were swollen too. They were very sick. I decided to make cuts where the fangs had sunk in and put a poultice on them. I killed some chickens, split them open and put their warm bodies on the cuts, hoping to draw out the poison."

"We don't know whether this really helped," Marguerite continued. "They were sick for a week or more and had trouble breathing. They wouldn't or couldn't eat. But gradually they got well."

"We wondered why all of them were bitten," Frenchy said. "We figured there must be a nest of snakes somewhere on the place. We had to find them before they got more livestock. We looked and looked for them and finally found a whole mass of snakes in a hole."

"Frenchy thought this discovery was unusual, and he decided to notify the Cheyenne newspaper," said Marguerite. "He rode to Horse Creek to phone them. They were interested and sent a photographer to take pictures. They took many pictures of the tangled mass of snakes. Then we dragged them all out of the hole. There were over ninety of them." Marguerite went over to a chest of drawers and took out a black and white picture postcard. She also had a clipping and picture from the newspaper. They had taken pictures of the snakes after they were dragged out of their nest too. They were horrible – all those snakes.

"How did you kill them?" Evelyn asked.

"We shot into the wriggling mass many times and used a hoe to kill the ones the bullets didn't kill," Frenchy said. "Most of them were small ones, but just think how dangerous our pastures would have been if they had all grown up and spread out all over the place."

"It was dangerous already," Marguerite said. "Our fine little colts are dead."

"At least we have our team. They can have more colts, Marguerite."

Evelyn and Pearl had to start back home early, because they wanted to be out of the hills before dark. When they went outside they saw the biggest cat they had ever seen. It was a tiger cat.

"What a beautiful cat," Pearl said.

"It's so huge now," Evelyn said. "The last time we were here it was only half grown and kind of skinny."

"This cat is a hunter," Frenchy bragged. "It lives the way God designed cats to live. It catches small animals for food. And would you believe it – it's a fisherman too. We've seen it pull trout out of the stream."

"But cats don't like water!" Pearl said. "How does it catch fish without getting wet?"

"Water doesn't bother this cat," Marguerite said proudly. "It pounces right on any unlucky fish it sees in the shallows. It's true, cats don't really like water, but remember they like fish very much."

Its diet and its outdoor life of complete freedom obviously agreed with this healthy animal. On their rides the girls had often seen their cat, Socks, sitting patiently by a gopher hole or rabbit burrow waiting to pounce. But he stayed close to home most of the time and liked to laze in the sun or by the fire. They thought of Socks as big and strong, but he could not measure up to this animal.

It was good to visit their friends. The girls urged them to come down to the homestead, but they did not come all summer. They had work to do and stock to take care of. There was no one to leave in charge while they visited. As the girls rode away they talked about what a lonely life they must lead so far away from the nearest neighbors. But they were young and in love. They lived surrounded by natural beauty. And they had each other.

20. Edna and Ruth

There was so little traffic on the road near the homestead that notice was taken of every car that drove by. Dirk always barked, running toward the road and protesting the intrusion.

As the day drew near when Edna and her friends were expected, the girls paid even more attention to the cars. At last a model T was spied chugging along slowly. As it drew closer they could see that there were three people in it. It turned into the road leading to the house. The children waved and shouted.

The car came to a stop and the passengers got out. Everyone hugged and kissed Edna and greeted her friends.

Pearl couldn't wait. "Edna, can I go with you? I've always wanted to see Yellowstone Park. You have room for me, don't you?"

"I hope you can take her, Edna. She wouldn't be any trouble to you. It would be a great experience for her," Marie said.

"I just can't," Edna said. "I'm still paying off my P.E.O. loans. I have barely enough for this trip. Everyone is paying her own way and sharing in the car expenses. Also the car has no trunk and you can see the luggage takes up a lot of space. Sorry, Pearl, I'd like to take you."

Marie put her arm around Pearl and gave her a hug. Pearl was very disappointed but tried not to show it. She had been sure that Edna would take her, because they were such good pals even though there was an eight year difference in their ages. Edna had come home often for weekends when she was in college, generally bringing friends with her. Pearl looked forward to these visits and had a lot of fun with the collegians.

"I thought Ruth would be here," Edna commented. "She said she'd be here this morning. I want to drive as far as we can today."

"She'll probably come soon," Marie prophesied.

However, lunchtime came and went, and Ruth still had not arrived.

While they sat around after lunch, Ruth drove in. "I started early but had a flat tire," she said. "I couldn't fix it so I had to wait until someone came along to help."

Edna related that she had driven through a rainstorm in Iowa and had got stuck in the gumbo. A farmer had to pull the car loose with his team. Then they waited at the farmhouse until the road dried.

"Our roads get slippery when it rains, Edna," Marie warned. "Then the cars slide in the ditch."

Evelyn said, "When Bill Eklund took us to Cheyenne for dinner and a show, we slid into the ditch twice. The rain made the roads slippery as glass."

"Fortunately it's not raining now," Edna said. "We must start. It doesn't get dark 'til late so we can make good progress. We'll see you again on our way home."

Pearl was sorry to see them go. For a short time four of the six sisters had been together. "When you come back can you and Ruth stay here while?" she asked.

"Yes, Pearl," Ruth assured her. "My summer school is over now. I have all my things in the car trunk. I am going to Colorado later to find a place to stay during the school year and to see about a job. But I'll stay here a while."

"I can stay for a while too, Pearl," Edna added.

Ruth put a bag in the back seat of the Ford and away they went.

21. The Flood

They were doing the washing down in the draw. They had to dip water out of the spring and carry it to the wash tub. The tub was perched atop rocks arranged in a ring around a fire.

Everyone helped with the washing. While they were down in the draw they took turns weeding the garden, picking peas and beans, and gathering other produce. Jackie picked a large bouquet of sweet peas for his mother.

Marie did the actual washing. She was very particular about it. In spite of the primitive facilities the clothes were washed very clean. All stains were scrubbed out of the garments and linens with Fels Naptha soap. The sound of rubbing and rubbing on the ridged washboard was continuous. Whites would later be boiled in a big copper boiler, and the strong Wyoming sun would further bleach them.

Evelyn and Pearl carried the first washed and rinsed clothes out of the deep draw and pinned them securely on the line. Clouds had been moving in and a very light rain had begun to fall, but they hung them up anyway, knowing that it would soon stop and the clothes would dry rapidly when the sun shone again.

They went back into the draw where Marie was continuing to wash. But suddenly Marie became alarmed when a stream of water appeared in the draw. Usually it was completely dry.

She knew what might happen. In arid lands where the vegetation is sparse and the soil is hard and absorbs little moisture, rainwater mostly runs off the land, seeking the lowest level. Sometimes crossing-places in a dry wash like the draw will flood even when no rain is falling at that spot. The rain may come from a far-off storm and thunder down in a wall of water many feet high. Unwary strangers in the country trying to ford such places may be swept away before they realize what is happening. Sometimes people even camp in these dry washes not realizing the danger. Generally, if you know the country you keep track of signs of storms in distant places. You can see a long way on the plains. But this time rain was everywhere and waters from distant places augmented the local rain which had increased in intensity. The water was rising very fast in the draw.

"Go to the house at once!" Marie shouted.

"Shall we carry the clothes with us?"

"No! Hurry! Go at once!" Marie picked up Jackie and stepped into the water. It was up to her knees by this time. The current was very strong, but she stumbled along doggedly. The girls joined hands and followed her. The water pushed against their legs. The soil and gravel under their feet seemed to be giving way. The rolling waters made them dizzy. Somehow they managed to stagger through and up the hill. The roar of the water was louder and louder. They were glad to reach the house and collapsed onto chairs.

"We should have stayed on the other side of the flood waters," Marie said. "We could have climbed to higher ground on that side and waited until the flood waters went down."

"Well, it never happened before," Evelyn said, defending her mother. "It's natural to make a dash for the house."

Marie shuddered. "I almost fell down, and Jackie

could have been torn from my arms."

"We're all safe anyway," Arlynn said.

"What about the clothes?" Pearl worried. "About half of our things are down there."

"And the garden," Evelyn said. "Will it be ruined?"

"We don't know. Probably the clothes will all wash away. The garden will suffer some damage. It depends on how deeply rooted the plants are. There is no use worrying about it. There is nothing we can do to save the clothes or the garden," Marie said calmly. "It's not important. We are safe."

Evelyn started for the door. "I'm going out to see how high the water is now."

"I am too."

"And I."

"Me too," said Jackie.

Marie let everyone go. The girls looked down into the draw to see how high the water was. It was very high now. They could not see the tubs or boiler. The garden was covered with water.

Jackie was not interested in the flood. He went around the other side of the house to look for his wagon. He ran back to the house shouting, "The chickens! The chickens!" He was holding two bedraggled chicks in his hands. The girls ran around the house and saw another disaster. Little chickens were drowning in the rivulets that ran through the yard. They all began picking them up, dashing here and there, and taking them into the house.

When it rained the hens did not have sense enough to call their chicks to them and go into the safety of the hen house. Since they ran free they were not close to it. They were scattered all over the yard.

"Build a small fire in the stove!" Marie ordered. "I'll fix a box for them." She put some clean rags in the bottom of a big dishpan. There was no box handy. Then she put the chicks in the pan and put it on the open oven door. When the chicks were warm some of them began moving. Their yellow down fluffed out. The smell of wet feathers was nauseating. Everyone could hardly wait until the ground dried so they could put them outside again. Many of the chicks did not revive. This was a big loss. The family depended upon the chickens for eggs and meat.

While they were busy with this emergency the rain continued. When they had done all they could they went over to the edge of the draw and peered down again. There was a raging torrent of water.

The water stayed in flood for about an hour. They checked on it from time to time. Finally they saw the garden. All the plants were flattened. Some rows had been washed away. Mud had washed over everything.

"We can replant some fast-growing things," Marie said. "Greens, onions, radishes, and maybe some other things. Some of the plants will straighten up and continue to grow. Maybe we will have to stake them up and pat some earth around their roots."

There was no sign of the washtub, boiler, or clothes. Even the stones upon which the tub full of clothes had rested had rolled away.

Arlynn said, "Let's ride out tomorrow – all three of us girls – and see if we can find any of the clothes."

"And the tub and boiler," Evelyn added.

The next day they rode down the draw. They did not find any clothes. At the boundary of the homestead where the fence was built down into the draw, some bits of cloth were hanging on the wreckage of the fence.

"Wow! Now we've got a new problem," Evelyn exclaimed. "This is the hardest kind of fencing job. We have to reset the posts on the steep sides of the draw.

We've got to put some very deep in the bottom of the draw and string up new barbed wire. Then we must wind wire around some large rocks and fasten them to the fence in the bottom of the draw to anchor it."

"Let's ride a few miles farther, on the Farthing range," Arlynn said. "Maybe we will find the tub or boiler."

They did not find either, so they turned home to report the damage to the fence. "The fence will have to be repaired at once," Marie said. "If some of the Farthing's huge herd of cattle come in here, they can consume more grass in a few hours than our stock does in months. If our stock gets onto their range-lands they would not like that either."

Marie had wire stretchers, a posthole digger, barbed wire, staples, hammers, and some extra fence posts. She and Evelyn knew how to put up a fence. This would be a big job. That very day they got everything together, piled it into the wagon and drove over there and fixed the fence. Pearl and Arlynn helped all they could. It took all day!

They had lost a lot of clothes, their washtub and boiler and washboard, some garden produce, and many little chickens. The fence had been damaged. And they had gained a greater respect for and fear of the destructive power of floods.

22. A Barn Dance

A cowboy on a fine horse stopped by one day. "Get down and sit awhile," Marie said – the usual western greeting to those on horseback.

"Sure. And I have good news for all of you. There's to be a barn dance at Iron Mountain this Saturday. Everyone is to spread the news. Have you heard about it?"

"No, we haven't. But we'll go, of course. It's always fun. The girls will enjoy the square dances and round dance."

"I don't know how to do that kind of dancing," Pearl said disappointedly. "I can fox trot and waltz, but I can't do that kind of dancing."

"It's easy to learn," Evelyn said. "The caller tells you what to do. We'll explain to you what all the calls mean. Anyway your partners will swing you around and set you on your way."

"Do young girls like us get to take part in these dances?" Pearl asked.

"Yes, anyone who wants to," the cowboy said. "Even little kids. And the older people especially enjoy it."

"Maybe I'll like it," Pearl said doubtfully.

"You will!" everyone chorused. "Wait and see. It's fun."

Pearl admired the cowboy's horse and wanted to ride it. It was about time to go after the cows for the evening milking. She asked the cowboy, "Can I ride your horse?" She was surprised to hear herself ask since she was usually very shy.

"Of course. He's a reliable, well-trained horse."

Pearl mounted the tall horse and felt proud as she cantered out of the yard. This was a real cow horse, not a child's pet.

When Pearl reached the cows and got around behind them the horse went into action, almost leaving her behind. He jumped back and forth urging the cows on, with no guidance from her. Pearl tried to slow him down, because milk cows must not run. It was hard to do. He'd dash over and lightly nip on the flank of any cow that stopped to graze. This horse was not used to driving in ambling milk cows. It was used to round-ups and cutting out stock for branding. Pearl was glad when she got back home. He was too much horse for her. Still, it was thrilling to ride such a horse.

The girls talked about the dance every day. On Saturday evening they did the chores, took baths in the new wash tub, and dressed in their best dresses. They seldom wore dresses so fortunately none of their dress-up clothes had been lost in the flood. They hitched the team to the two-wheeled cart and saddled two ponies. Only three people could ride in the cart. Evelyn and Pearl tucked up their skirts as best they could and rode ponies.

When they got to Iron Mountain there were some horses and quite a few cars there. Others soon arrived. The barn was lighted with lanterns, and bales of hay were arranged around the walls so people would have a place to sit. An old-fashioned fiddler was swaying away vigorously. The loud, rhythmic chant of the caller directed the movements of a crowd of bobbing and whirling dancers. "Swing that lady high and low." "Do-see-do." "Allemande left your corners all." "Now promenade partners half-way round." These and many other calls were instantly obeyed. It all looked confusing to Pearl, and she decided not even to try dancing.

Babies were sleeping on blankets spread out on the hay. As the evening wore on small children fell asleep one by one.

The dancing crowd was made up of all ages and all types of people. Frontier society is a democratic society. People are judged on their real merits, not according to their wealth or their family. Friendliness, honesty and helpfulness were the criteria by which people were evaluated. There were ranch hands and ranchers and homesteaders and their families. The men who worked at the quarry were there too.

Before the evening was over all of them were dancing, including Pearl. It was true; the neophytes were guided by the others. It was really not difficult. The dancing continued all night long. People would dance, then rest a while and visit and then continue dancing. Everyone had brought food along. When they stopped for refreshments people watched to see who was courting whom as couples paired off.

Sometimes trouble threatened. Some of the young men brought along flasks of whiskey. They would go outside, drink too much and become quarrelsome. A fight would break out. Older, more responsible men would break up the fight and send these show-offs home or at least tell them they could not enter the barn again. There were no drunken dancers.

This was in the twenties, the Prohibition Era, when the manufacturing, transportation and sale of alcoholic beverages was against the law. Bootlegging, the illegal distilling and sale of intoxicating liquors, was common. Many men carried a flask in their hip pockets.

People began to look and feel tired. In the grey light of early morning they started drifting away. Marie had to get home to milk the cows on time and feed the chickens and pigs. So she called the children together, and they began the long, slow ride home. Their heads were nodding. It did not matter that they were very sleepy. The horses knew the way and were eager to get there.

When they arrived they unhitched the team and turned them loose. Marie went into the kitchen, built a fire and prepared breakfast. Evelyn and Pearl took off their party clothes, put on riding clothes and went after the cows. Then they turned their ponies loose, did the milking, took care of the milk, fed the chickens and pigs, ate breakfast and went to bed.

They slept soundly in the apartment until the middle of the afternoon. However, Jackie had slept all night on a bale of hay, and when he got home he was ready to play. Marie did not get much rest until the girls got up. Evelyn and Pearl went after the wild ponies and worked with Midget and Prince until it was time to do the evening chores.

23. The Return

The evening chores were finished, and Marie was reading Owen Wister's novel, *The Virginian*, aloud to the children. It was a wonderful story about a tenderfoot in Wyoming. There was a lot of humor in it.

Dirk rushed to the door, barking furiously. They went outside and saw a car coming slowly toward the house. It was Edna's car. Everyone crowded around it as it came to a stop.

Greetings were exchanged with Edna, Ruth, Hortense and Mrs. Warman. Then Marie asked, "Where is the top of the car?"

"The wind blew it off," Edna said, laughing. Something seemed to be written on the side in white. The girls investigated the messages.

"It says 'The Spirit of St. Vitus' on this side," Arlynn yelled.

"On the back the message is 'Yellowstone or Bust!'" Pearl reported.

"I can't read what is written on this side," Evelyn said, "It's smudged."

"Did you have fun?" Marie inquired.

"The whole trip was great," Ruth said. "Yellowstone Park is so beautiful."

The travelers told about the lake, the falls on the river, the canyon, the hot springs, and Old Faithful.

Edna said, "Some people think Wyoming is just flat, treeless prairies, but they should see the beautiful mountains, the lodge pole pines, the lakes that we saw. Wyoming is wonderful."

"Did you have any car trouble, flats, or blowouts?" Marie asked.

"No tire trouble. I bought new tires before leaving home."

"It's lucky we didn't have tire trouble," Ruth stated. "None of us has ever changed a tire or mended an inner tube."

Edna laughed. "If we'd had problems, we would have gotten out of the car and stood there looking helpless. We might even have used our handkerchiefs and pretended to be crying."

"Everybody seemed to get a kick out of our roofless, dilapidated car with the silly signs on it," Ruth commented. "People were very nice to us."

The others chimed in: "That's true." "They really were." "Very helpful and friendly."

"Come on in the house now," Marie said. "You must be tired and thirsty. Maybe hungry too. We'll help you move your things in."

After they carried the luggage in, Pearl asked, "Did you see any bears?"

Edna looked accusingly at the others. They seemed somewhat abashed. "We saw plenty of bears!" she exclaimed. "I'll tell you about one that I saw too close up! We stopped, and I got out of the car to take a picture of one on the road. While I was taking the picture the bear began ambling toward the car. I heard someone shout, 'He's coming. Drive away.' And away they went, leaving me on foot, with the bear between me and the car."

The others looked sheepish but seemed to be suppressing embarrassed laughter.

"Well, Edna, the bear was coming toward the car," Ruth said defensively. "It could climb right in. Then you wouldn't have wanted to get in, would you?"

"All I know is you deserted me," Edna accused.

"Well, anyway we didn't drive too far," Hortense reminded Edna. "When we drove away the bear started toward another car that had stopped and you made it to the car safely."

"No thanks to you!" Edna was still indignant. She could not see anything funny about the incident.

"Did the bear get you, Edna?" Jackie asked. The girls began to giggle.

Marie hastily changed the subject. "What other animals did you see?"

"We saw mountain sheep way off in the distance, high up on a mountain," Ruth reported. "We saw a moose standing in a boggy meadow. Driving south through Jackson Hole we saw elk. And we saw deer and many bands of American antelope on the way to the park."

"People tell me that there used to be antelope and deer around here," Marie interjected. "I guess we are too close to Cheyenne. Hunters must have killed them all or driven them out."

"I wish they were still here," Pearl stated. "They are pretty and graceful. I saw some antelope from the train window as we went through Nebraska. Some people on the train thought they were goats."

"Didn't you have trouble getting up steep mountain grades, Edna?" Marie asked.

"We crawled up in low. The engine would overheat, and we'd have to stop until it cooled off," Edna reported. "Then we had to set the spark and crank the car to get started again."

"It's amazing that such a car could make it in the mountains," Marie commented.

"Well, it quivered and shook and groaned, but we got there and back with no trouble," Edna bragged.

"We had a flood in the draw while you were gone

and lost all the clothes we were washing," Arlynn reported.

"You missed a lot of fun," Evelyn said. "We went to a barn dance last week."

These events were reported in detail to the travelers. Then Hortense said, "Marie, Edna told me how you started homesteading when Evelyn was just a little girl. Weren't you scared and lonely?"

Marie assured her that she was not afraid. Homesteading was something she very much wanted to do. She answered several questions about her experiences. Then she addressed Edna. "Edna, when you are here at the homestead does it come back to you how you helped me deliver Jackie?" Marie asked.

"You delivered a baby here?" Hortense was amazed.

Edna nodded. "I did. I had to. I was only seventeen years old. I had arrived here the very day that Jackie was born. When I got off the train at Altus, there was no one there to meet me."

"That was terrible, Edna. I went to the hills with Jack to gather wood. I always wanted to go everywhere with him," Marie explained. "We didn't know we would be gone so long."

Mrs. Warman asked, "Wasn't it risky for you to ride up into the hills in a jolting wagon when you were so far along in your pregnancy?"

"The baby wasn't expected for several weeks. Probably the jolting had a lot to do with Jackie's arrival that night. Edna, you tell what happened."

"There were box cars at Altus with railroad workers living in them. The women living there welcomed me to stay until Jack and Marie came after me."

"Edna, how did you know what to do when the baby was born?" Hortense asked. "Of course, Jack was there to help you, wasn't he?"

"No, he wasn't," Edna said. "When Marie's pains began he ran all the way to Altus to phone the doctor. That was quicker than getting a horse. He had arranged ahead of time for a doctor and nurse to come from Cheyenne. But they got lost and didn't find the homestead 'til morning when everything was all over. Mother was afraid that the baby might be born before the doctor arrived. Both Evelyn and Arlynn were born before the doctor arrived. So she told me a few things – how to tie the cord and care for Marie. I didn't know anything about how babies were born. Mother also packed some needed supplies in my trunk. But the trunk didn't arrive when I did."

"Of course, I was conscious the whole time and could give her advice," Marie added.

"Weren't you scared almost to death, Edna?" Pearl asked.

"I was, but everything depended on me. I had to take charge. I couldn't believe what was happening. Mother had not really told me what to expect."

"Well, if you had lived on a ranch and had seen calves and foals born you wouldn't have been surprised," Evelyn interrupted.

"Marie didn't have any anesthetic," Edna said. "It was hard for her. She tried not to cry out, because she knew I was scared."

Marie added, "Fortunately there were no complications. It was a normal delivery, and the baby was strong and healthy. I was so happy about that. I had had a miscarriage a year before, and the baby, a little boy, died. So I was afraid I might lose this child too."

"The baby cried loudly and kicked hard," Edna said. "I could tell when I held him in my arms from the way he squirmed that he was okay. Both of us thought he looked like Jack."

"I know you cannot really tell who a small baby resembles, but we did agree on that," Marie said. "And as you can see Jackie is a perfect little Dutchman. He does look like Jack, yellow curly hair, blue eyes, his features. I will show you a picture of Jack, and you can see for yourself. He certainly doesn't look like anyone on my side of the family." Marie brought out a photo album. It was passed around and everyone agreed that Jackie looked like his father.

"Edna, tell about your other frightening experience here," Ruth suggested.

"I remember that vividly," Edna said. "I slept on a cot here in the kitchen. One night I was awakened by the sound of someone moving about in the room. I was just ready to speak when a match was struck, and I could see the face of a strange man. He was lighting a cigarette. At first I was paralyzed with fright. I wanted to scream and to run to Marie. But I could not make a sound or move. Finally I forced a scream out of my dry throat and called as loudly as I could, 'Jack! Jack!' He heard me at once and came bounding out to confront the man. It turned out that he wasn't dangerous. He was just traveling through the country alone, and he was tired, cold, and hungry. He meant to rouse us and ask for food and a hot drink."

Many questions came from the listeners. "Why didn't he knock?" "Wasn't the door locked?" "Did you give him something to eat?" "What if Jack hadn't been there?"

Marie responded, "No one out here locks a door. We don't have any locks or keys. It would be useless anyway. If someone wanted to come in, it would be easy to break down the door or come in through a window. Yes, he was armed, but men here usually carry a revolver. This is still a kind of frontier country, and it is understood that any stranger will be welcomed and helped. This man should have knocked and roused us. I don't know why he didn't. Maybe he thought we were not at home. In that case, it is all right to go in, rest and eat whatever you can find. No one would begrudge providing food for a hungry man. You might well need food and shelter yourself sometime. You have seen how far apart the ranches, homesteads and little towns are. There are only eighty-some towns in all of Wyoming, a state that comes close to being twice as big as Iowa or Illinois."

"And many of those towns have very few people," Ruth added.

"Some places that were named on our map had only a store," Hortense said. "They weren't really towns. Only one family lived in some of them."

"We were really glad to come to one of those places," Ruth interjected. "We were always afraid of running out of gas before we could get to the next town. We could always buy something to eat too."

"Where did you stay at night?" Arlynn asked.

"In little tourist cabins," Edna answered. "They are tiny. They aren't like hotels. There are no bathrooms, no running water. Just a place to sleep. We had to take sponge baths and go to an outhouse."

They talked until late. Then Marie told the girls to move their bedding onto the floor of the apartment so the guests and Edna could have their cots. Ruth would sleep with her.

In the morning Pearl and Evelyn brought in the ponies and demonstrated how they were training them.

Marie asked if anyone would like to ride horseback.

"Do you have some gentle horses, Marie?" Hortense asked.

"Yes, Headlight and Baldy are very reliable. I'll ride Smoky and go along with you."

Mrs. Warman and Ruth didn't want to ride. Evelyn surprised the family by telling Edna she should ride Waltina.

Evelyn and Pearl rode two of the ponies they were training and got the horses in.

Smoky acted up when Marie got on him. Hortense was scared but soon realized that Marie could control him.

Edna, Marie and Hortense rode up into the breaks, and Marie showed Hortense where the Indians used to camp. Then they rode down into the draw and meandered through it all the way back to the house, pausing to see the spring and the garden.

They rested, ate lunch, and Hortense and Mrs. Warman packed their suitcases. Edna drove them to Altus to catch the train to Cheyenne. Arlynn and Jackie went along for the ride.

24. A Letter Home

Dear Mother and Dad,

I'm sorry I haven't written to you oftener. We are so busy training the ponies and doing chores that I don't have much time. Actually we are busy having a good time too.

We went to a barn dance and danced all night. There wasn't any ballroom dancing – just square dancing and other country dances. It was fun.

The Dunns drove out and persuaded Marie to visit them for a day or two. She will buy some clothes and sheets in Cheyenne to replace those we lost in the flood. Arlynn and Jackie went with Marie. They'll come back on the train.

I'm glad you can come out for the big rodeo in Cheyenne, Mother. The Dunns have invited us to stay with them. Evelyn and I plan to ride to Cheyenne and take along an extra horse for Christina. It will be a long ride, about 35 miles, but we can do it in one day.

The ponies we are working with now are Midget and Prince. Midget is black; Prince is black and white. Prince is named after the Welsh pinto you drove when I was a small child. He's beautiful. I can't wait until you see the ponies; they are so pretty. Of course, some have already been sold, much to our sorrow.

When Marie left, Evelyn and I decided to do all the chores conscientiously, work with the ponies several hours, and then read all day. We wouldn't cook; we would just eat canned peaches with whipped cream. Fruit is something we don't get much of here. Peaches with our thick, rich whipped cream sounded like heaven. They tasted so good. At first! Then not quite so delicious but okay. Then we gagged at the thought of them. Now we are eating fresh garden produce, oatmeal, eggs, meat – no sweets.

We rode to the store at Horse Creek yesterday and bought a few things. Really we just felt lonesome without the others and wanted to see someone. We stopped at the Inness ranch just this side of Horse Creek and visited with the girls and Mr. and Mrs. Inness. They are such fine people.

I found out recently that they lost their only son when he was struck by lightning as he walked from the barn to the house. So terrible! He was in his teens, I think.

About a week ago a very old, bowlegged, wizened cowboy stopped in for a visit. His name is Angus MacDonald. He stayed for dinner. He's a well-known character in these parts. He could not believe that we were all drinking milk. Milk is for "damned calves." We had gelatin for dessert. When it was put before him, sparkling and quivering, he said, "Shake, damn you, shake! You aren't half as afraid of me as I am of you!" He's really amusing.

Some of the boys from the quarry drove us to Laramie to see Ruth. I think several of them are interested in Ruth, but now she has a handsome boyfriend there at school. We saw the university campus and drove up into the Snowy Range for a picnic. The mountains are beautiful. We took along some fishing equipment and a skillet, lard, and some corn meal to fry the fish if we caught any. We weren't depending on luck though. Just in case, we also had a hearty picnic lunch.

Nobody was catching any fish. Finally Evelyn tried one of the Indian ways of catching trout. Trout like to lie quiet under a cut bank when they aren't feeding. She looked for such places, moving quietly. When she saw a likely place she lay down and reached under the bank and grabbed at a fish. She caught several although more got away. She had to be very quick and hold on tightly. Otherwise slippery fish can wriggle out of your hand. None of the rest would even try to catch fish this way.

The rainbow trout are beautiful with tiny colored specks along their sides. The meat is delicious, crisp, and firm. They are appetizing because they live in the pure, cold mountain stream.

Wild roses are blooming in the draw. Evelyn and I have been gathering petals and drying them so we can make sachets. We'll have some for you to put with your clothes when you arrive.

This letter is too long. Well, we have a lot of time on our hands right now.

See you in July, Mother.

Love,

Pearl

P.S. I didn't get this mailed right away. Marie is home now. When she saw all the peach cans, she opened another one and served peaches and cream for dessert that night. Two of the diners didn't eat any!

P.P.S. Edna has gone to Laramie and to Cheyenne to visit friends quite often. I'm trying to persuade her to stay until the first week of September so I can ride home in her car. That would be fun, and it would save money too.

25. Haying

A neighboring rancher stopped in one day. After visiting a while he said, "We start haying next week. We need more help. Would any of you young people like a job?"

"Pearl and I would," Evelyn said. "You'd like to earn some money, wouldn't you, Pearl? Can we go, Mom?"

Marie thought a while before answering, "I think we can manage without you for a while. Arlynn could help with the milking."

"It will take about a week to get the hay in. My wife and I will take good care of the girls, Mrs. Achttien. Of course, they'll stay in the big house with us."

"I know they will be safe with you. What exactly will they do?"

"We thought Evelyn could drive the hay rake. That's safer than the mower. We know Evelyn is used to horses. Ranch kids can easily drive a rake. And Pearl can drive the stacker team."

The rancher told us to report for work. The haying was all done by *real* horse power. It involved much hard work. A horse-drawn mower was used to cut the hay. The hay would be left in the field until dry, and then raked into rows with a horse-drawn rake. Next, men would load it onto a flat wagon bed with pitchforks and drive to the barn. There it was loaded onto a horse-drawn lift and lifted to the haymow in the barn, where it would be spread around with pitchforks.

The girls arrived at the ranch late in the afternoon the day before they were to begin work. They took care of their ponies and turned them loose. The rancher's wife showed them to their room and told them that dinner would soon be ready.

The haying crew consisted of four men besides the ranch owner. There were eight people around the table. There was no talking; the table was heaped with food and eating was serious business.

As Pearl and Evelyn left the table the rancher's wife said, "You'll want to go to bed early, girls, because we get up before daybreak. Will you catch your ponies in the morning and bring in the horses for us?"

"Yes, we'll do that," Evelyn said. "We always take a pan of oats to make it easier to catch them. Do you have any oats?"

"Yes, in the barn. I'll show you where."

On the way to the barn the rancher's wife said, "I wish Marie could have come to cook for us. She did one year. She's a great cook. It would be nice to have her here for company too. But we know that she can't leave her homestead."

In the morning Pearl and Evelyn caught their ponies and brought in the draft horses. They turned the ponies loose and went in for breakfast. Pearl had never seen such a breakfast: beefsteak, hash browned potatoes, fried eggs, baked beans, bread and butter, jam and strong coffee. The first morning the girls ate dainty portions. The next day and every day after that they ate plenty of everything. Their work took a lot of energy, and they had ravenous appetites.

Pearl's job required walking back and forth all day, driving the stacker team. When she drove the team away from the barn the loaded lift was raised by ropes and pulleys to the large opening in the gable end of the hayloft. When it was emptied she drove the team back toward the barn to lower it for another load. And so on –

all day long, except for a rest and a meal at lunchtime.

Evelyn's job in the field required greater skill. She had to guide the horses just so, to make neat rows of hay. But she could sit down even though the seat on the rake was hard metal.

The men with the pitchforks had the hardest job. They were afoot and had to lift the hay onto the wagon all day. Then they had to pitch it onto the hay lift. And in the stifling heat of the barn loft a man spread the hay around evenly.

Everyone got very tired, and soon after cleaning up and having dinner the workers went to the bunkhouse. Everyone went to bed early. They would start again at dawn the next day to take advantage of the cool air of the morning.

Pearl and Evelyn earned some money and were very proud to be a part of a haying team. It was an interesting experience for a city girl. Pearl caught a glimpse into one aspect of life on a big ranch. Still she was glad when the week was over, and they returned home.

26. Letter to Ruth

Homestead

Dear Ruth,

Phebe and Teague are here now. Phebe had a spat with Teague and drove all the way up here from Texas with the children. Teague lost no time in coming after her; in fact he was here before she arrived. He loves his family very much. They want to see you, so do come this weekend if you can. CoNett and Jimmy are so cute.

A young steer was killed and butchered this week. I stayed indoors, because I didn't want to see any of it. I heard a shot ring out as I was walking across the kitchen and instinctively glanced out the window. The poor thing was staggering. I am now a vegetarian. There are plenty of eggs, and I can drink milk.

The carcass is hanging in a screened enclosure in the shade of the house. Marie says it will keep well in the cool, dry wind while some of it is used and the rest cold-packed for the winter.

I know that farmers and ranchers don't raise cattle for pets. It's just that I don't like to think of animals in connection with meat. I try to think of just steaks, chops, etc.

Ruth, bring your boyfriend when you come. We all like him.

Last night Evelyn and I carried a mattress out to the wagon and slept out. The stars were beautiful, and the air was crisp and cold. Jackie wanted to sleep outside too so he joined us. In the night it began to rain. We hurried to carry the mattress in. It was hard to hold onto with our sleep-weakened hands. We could just barely keep it off the ground. Jackie asked, "Can I ride on it?" Then we burst into laughter and got weaker still.

Ruth, a sheepherder drove his flock along the road through the homestead yesterday. It was a big flock. He came to the house to get permission. I don't know where he came from. The ranchers around here hate sheep. It was interesting to see the dogs work. They kept the sheep off the grass.

See you soon, I hope.

Love,

Pearl

P.S. Henry Braun came by the other day when we were working with the ponies. He asked us if he could ride one of our horses. We suggested that he ride Headlight or Baldy. He refused to ride a big horse and as usual chose Pal, because he is smaller.

As usual, Pal threw him off every time he tried to ride him. We tried to keep from laughing, but it was funny. How does Pal know he can do this with Henry? You have to admire Henry's persistence! Does he persist like this in proposing to you? Maybe you'll agree some day.

Henry was a German immigrant who had a homestead in Nebraska. He came to Wyoming each summer and worked at the quarry to earn money to improve his homestead. He asked around to see if someone would teach him English, and Ruth's name was suggested. Even though she showed absolutely no interest in him, he eventually made a very unromantic proposal. He told her that she wouldn't have to do any outdoor work – just keep house and cook for him. Ruth told the family about this, and the young, merciless girls had many a laugh about it. They loved to tease Ruth.

Henry was smart to emphasize that she wouldn't have to do chores. I could not imagine Ruth living her life on a homestead. She was very much the lady and loved to dress up. She didn't really even like to ride horseback. She had a Chevy coupe and preferred to drive a car.

The family respected Henry for his ambition and earnestness. Probably he became a rich successful man in his new country. He must have learned to speak good English and to ride horseback, because he had what it takes to succeed: a refusal to give up.

27. Phebe and Teague

Phebe and Teague stayed at the homestead through the weekend so they could see Ruth.

Everyone enjoyed having them on the homestead. No one mentioned the quarrel. That was something for the young couple to work out by themselves. Anyway it seemed to have been forgotten.

Pearl liked Teague very much. He understood children and knew how to entertain them. She remembered how he helped take care of his daughter and son when they were tiny babies and the family lived in Cedar Rapids. Whenever she thought of him, she pictured him carrying a child or patiently rocking a sleeping baby. She smiled to herself remembering how he sang to the babies in an absolute monotone, making up words of a lullaby. The family used to be amused by his unmelodic songs, but they loved to watch him with his children.

That evening when all had gathered together after chores, Pearl asked Teague, "Do you remember what I said to you when I first met you?"

"I'll never forget that, Pearl. It really pleased me." He addressed the group, "She said she missed her father. He was working in Oklahoma City, and the family hadn't moved there yet. She asked me if I would be like a father to Arlynn and her. It was a special welcome into the family. I hadn't met any of Phebe's family before except Marie and Evelyn and Jack."

"We used to play cards a lot at Mother's house," Phebe recalled. "The popular game then was five hundred."

"And go on picnics at Ellis Park," Pearl said. "We swam at the public beach on the river. I wish you lived in Cedar Rapids now." Pearl thought a moment and added, "Teague, didn't you first meet Phebe in Wyoming? How did you happen to come here?"

"My brother Bill had a homestead in the hills. I came here to see him."

"He was the foreman of the Y Cross ranch," Phebe said. "I had come out with a neighbor girl to work on the ranch."

"Bill was Jack's and my friend," Marie added. "When he sold his homestead, he gave us a lot of things."

"Phebe, tell us about your first meeting with Teague," Evelyn urged.

"It was New Year's Eve in 1920. Bill and his girlfriend and all the help at the ranch went to Horse Creek to meet him. There was a blizzard, and we got there at the last minute."

"I wouldn't have got off the train if I hadn't seen them there," Teague said. "It was such a God-forsaken looking spot. But the minute I got off the train and saw Phebe I made up my mind that she was the girl I was going to marry. She was beautiful, with golden hair and big blue eyes, but even more wonderful, she was full of fun and laughter. I was ready to marry. I'd been in the trenches in France. I was gassed over there. I wanted to have a wife and children and forget about the war."

"Did Teague actually propose to you that first night, Phebe?" Pearl asked. Like all young girls she liked romantic stories.

"Yes, he did. Within a week we decided to get married. I went home to get ready for the wedding, and he returned to Texas. We wrote every day. Then he asked me to come to Fort Worth for the wedding. We were married there in a minister's home. Then we went to a backwoods area to live near some of Teague's relatives. His parents were dead. It was a terrible place. There were spiders and snakes, no running water. I had to do the washing in a pond under a bridge and hang the clothes on a fence. The people there didn't treat me well. Women were considered inferior. Very few women there could call their souls their own. Dad had taken a job in Oklahoma City. He came to Fort Worth on a business trip in June. I met him there and went home with him. That's why we moved to Cedar Rapids. I went up there at once. We stayed there several years. Teague had a job as manager of a Piggly Wiggly store there. When we moved back to Texas, we lived in town. I had many nice friends and liked it there. I'm a real Texan now," Phebe said.

Pearl listened eagerly to this story. She liked the whirlwind romance. She could not understand the adjustments which marriage required. In stories people lived happily ever after – no problems.

"Texans just can't stay away from Texas," Teague said.

"Teague, when you return home, tell Bill hello for me," Marie said. "He was a good friend. He was here when Evelyn and I moved into this shack. I wasn't married to Jack yet. The tar paper wasn't nailed onto the outside, and the snow blew in through the cracks. Bill and some others had brought wood and piled it up near the house so we could keep warm."

"Marie, why didn't you wait until summer?" Phebe asked. "It must have been very lonely for you."

"I wanted to be in my own home. I was happy here."

"Will you sell your homestead someday?" Phebe inquired.

"Never. I love it here."

"It's such a hard life, especially in winter," Ruth

said. "Maybe, someday, Marie, you will decide to leave."

"I don't think so, but I suppose we don't really know what we'll do in the future. When I was growing up in Iowa, I never dreamed I'd be a homesteader in Wyoming."

"Phebe, I wish we had a piano here so you could play for us," Pearl said. "Remember how we had a music room in Mt. Vernon and how we gathered around the piano and sang? A lot of the songs were World War songs. I still remember those old songs. 'Goodbye Ma, Goodbye Pa, goodbye mule with your old hee haw, I don't quite know what the war's about, but I bet by gosh I'll soon find out'."

"And It's a Long, Long Way to Tipperary," Ruth said. "And They're All Out of Step But Jim. And Over There."

"I liked The Dark Town Strutters' Ball and K-k-k-katy," Evelyn said.

"Marie, you should have a Victrola," Teague said. "Then you'd have music when you want it."

"I just don't have money for anything extra. I must save so I can buy hay and feed for winter."

"Someday I hope you can get a phonograph," Phebe said.

"Why don't we sing some of those old songs?" Pearl suggested. They sang several songs, Phebe giving the pitch.

"Phebe, I remember how thrilled I was when you took me to see my first movie in Mt. Vernon. The movie was in a vacant store – just a screen, projector and some straight chairs. You played the piano, and I sat on the piano bench beside you. The movies were silent then. That is, the actors and actresses couldn't be heard talking, but there was *music* so they weren't totally silent. You played soft, sentimental music for the love scenes and loud, thundering music for stormy scenes."

Pearl was happy. Four of her sisters and her brother-in-law were here with her. She was glad she had come to Wyoming. She knew she would see her other sister Betty often during the school year, because Cornell College was only fourteen miles from home. She thought to herself how she would get everyone to contribute money to buy Marie a Victrola for Christmas. She could earn her share by babysitting.

28. An All Day Ride

It was the middle of July, and Cheyenne Frontier Days would soon begin. The girls worked harder with the ponies. They were training the last three – Pronto, Misty, and Star. Pronto was a very lively bay and white pinto, Misty was grey, and Star was black with a white star on her face. Whang, Midget, and Prince had to be ridden every day too, to maintain their training. Arlynn and Jackie were a big help in riding the tamer ponies.

As Pearl and Evelyn worked with the ponies they were planning their trip to Cheyenne. They discussed what to wear and what to take along. Also they had to decide what horses to take. It was taken for granted that Evelyn would ride Waltina. Pearl decided to ride Pal, because he was a lively and willing pony. They settled on taking Tiny for Christine Dunn.

Anyone who rode a horse was admitted free. Riders could go into the area behind the chutes where they could see the contestants get onto the broncs or Brahma bulls in the narrow chutes. Then the gate would be opened, and the animals would come charging out, trying every gyration that might throw the rider.

The girls wanted to ride in the parade. Cowboys and cowgirls from Wyoming and states close by and the professional rodeo contestants would be in the parade. The professionals wore elaborate and expensive boots, chaps, and hats. They wore fancy silk shirts and bright colored scarves. Indians always had a large encampment near the rodeo grounds. They dressed in tribal clothes and rode in the parade. Cavalrymen from Fort

Warren would be there on their beautiful sleek horses.

Evelyn and Pearl planned their trip carefully. They would wear, as always, their ten gallon hats to protect them from the fierce sun. They would wear cowgirl boots, of course. These were made of fine, soft leather, fitting like a glove over the instep and flaring at the top. They had fancy stitching on the sides. The heels were high enough so the rider's foot would not slip through the stirrup if he kept his heel down as a rider should. They would wear riding pants and western style shirts.

They would stop only once, at Federal, approximately the half-way point. They hoped to be there by lunchtime. There was only a store with attached living quarters there. The couple who ran it, the Schwatkes, were friends. The girls would buy things for lunch there and unsaddle the horses, water them and let them graze awhile.

The day of departure they got up very early, caught their horses and brought in the cows. Then they breakfasted and left. Marie and Arlynn would milk all the cows. They took along a few snacks and the clothes they would need.

They walked and trotted the horses. Thirty-five miles was a long ride. Now and then they would ride Tiny and lead one of their horses. Sometimes they dismounted and walked awhile so they would not get so stiff. The road was gravel. Several times they inspected the horses' hooves to be sure that no stones were lodged in them.

They saw very few cars. There was only one ranch after they passed the Inness ranch. This was King Merritt's ranch, a very large spread. The big house was set back some distance from the road. There were trees around it, and it looked very fine. Grass and trees can be grown in Wyoming if they are watered.

They met a sheepherder driving some angora sheep or goats on the road near the ranch house. This breed had long, silky hair, not tightly-curled hair like the usual breed in the West.

The ride became very monotonous. They fell silent thinking of the miles ahead of them. Only the creak of the saddles could be heard. They changed positions in the saddle, sometimes putting a leg over the saddle horn. At last they reached Federal. They unsaddled their horses and went inside the store.

Mrs. Schwatke said, "What are you doing so far from home, girls?"

"We're going to Cheyenne to see the rodeo and ride in the parade," Evelyn said.

"Why the pack horse?"

"We're taking an extra pony along for a friend, Christine Dunn," Pearl said.

"We know the Dunns. They usually stop here," Mr. Schwatke commented. "It's a long ride. I hope you get there before dark." He looked at this watch. "It's two o'clock now."

"How is Marie?" Mrs. Schwatke asked.

"She's fine," answered Evelyn. "Everything is going well on the homestead. We did lose a lot of clothes in a flood a while back."

"Your mother told us about that when she went in to Cheyenne to shop," Mrs. Schwatke said.

"Can we give our horses some water?" Pearl asked.

The Schwatke's helped water the horses. The girls left them to graze while they went inside to eat. The horses were hungry and tired. With the reins down they would not move far. Pearl and Evelyn were tired and stayed there quite a while, then they resumed their ride. In about an hour the sky became cloudy and a sudden rainstorm soaked them. Their boots filled with water.

The road became slick. Just as suddenly the rain stopped and the sun came out. They took off their boots and dumped the water out. Then they tied them to the saddle upside down, hoping they would dry out. Their clothes dried quickly in the sun and wind and after a while the boots were dry too.

Several times deer flies attacked their horses. These are large, speckled, brownish flies. They go right into a horse's nostril and bite. The horse goes wild. The girls dismounted and killed the flies. It was difficult to do but worth the effort. The sun sank below the horizon, and they rode on in the twilight. They had no way of knowing how far they still had to go. It got almost dark, and they still were not there. Finally they saw the city lights so they knew they were near. When they reached the Dunn's it was dark. Their friends said they had worried about them.

They helped the girls take care of the horses. Christine was glad that they had brought Tiny for her to ride. Pearl was happy to learn that her mother would come in on the train the next day.

29. Unexpected Opportunity

Evelyn and Pearl and their horses had a day to rest before the Frontier Days rodeo began. A friend of the Dunns was arranging the amateur events. He drove to the house that evening and met Evelyn and Pearl.

"Why don't you girls ride in the calf riding event? I have a few boys signed up but would like to have some girls ride too."

"Can we, Dad?" Christine asked.

"You'll have to clear it with your mother."

"Mother, can we ride?"

"Well, I guess it would be all right for you to ride, Christine. But I can't give permission to Pearl and Evelyn. We'll have to see what Pearl's mother says about it."

"Grandma will think it's all right," Evelyn said.

"Yes, she'll let us ride," Pearl said.

"We must wait and see," Nonnie Dunn insisted.

"When does your mother arrive?" the man asked.

"Tonight," Pearl answered. "We'll call you as soon as we know."

When Pearl's mother arrived the girls besieged her with reasons why they should be allowed to ride.

"We've been riding wild ponies all summer," Pearl said. "It'll be easy to ride a calf."

"Grandma, we don't have to ride very long."

"There will be cowboys there to help us get on," Pearl added. "And there will be ropes around the calves for us to hang onto."

"Christine's mother says she can ride," Evelyn said.

"Yes, of course you can ride if the Dunns think it's safe."

The girls breathed a sigh of relief. "Thank you, Mother." "Thank you, Grandma."

The next evening a car drove up to the house. Arlynn got out. "I couldn't wait to see Mother!" she exclaimed. Arlynn called her grandmother "Mother" because she had brought her up and didn't go to Wyoming to live until she reached her teens. She had been with her mother only during infrequent vacation visits. Arlynn's grandmother loved her dearly. "And I wanted to see the rodeo, so Marie said I could come in with Bill."

"Arlynn, the girls want to ride calves in the rodeo. Do you want to too?"

"Oh, yes. I do!"

Naomi Dunn telephoned the promoter and told him about Arlynn and he said he would put their names on the program. Then he said, "I'm coming over right away. I have another idea that I want to talk over with you."

Soon he appeared. He was introduced to Mother and said, "It's you I want to talk to. I can see that your granddaughter Evelyn is a strong young ranch girl. I know she rides every day and has even been breaking ponies this summer. My idea is this. I'd like to have her ride a Brahma bull in the rodeo. We've never had a girl rider."

"Aren't those the great big bulls with humps on their backs?" Mother said. "Those bulls charge at the fallen riders. She could get trampled or gored."

Naomi said, "There are two clowns who distract the bull to keep it away from the rider 'til he can climb the fence, but something could go wrong. The bulls have long, sharp horns. They're dangerous."

"Your granddaughter won't have to climb the

fence," the promoter said. "We'll have two pick-up men on fast horses. If it looks as though she's losing her seat the nearest one will dash up and lift her onto his horse. The men ride the bulls until they fall off or jump off. We don't intend to let Evelyn fall off. If she should, the two riders will go in and protect her and one will pick her up. The clowns will be there too."

"Please, Grandma, I want to do it," Evelyn said. "I'm not afraid."

"I know your granddaughter is an excellent rider. I've heard all about her."

"She is," Mother said. "She's a wonderful rider. I think she can do it." Mother always believed that her children could do anything. This supreme confidence in their abilities extended to her grandchildren as well.

"Thanks, Grandma."

The girls were so proud. They would be contestants in the rodeo, not mere spectators. But Pearl secretly worried about Evelyn riding a Brahma bull. Pearl knew that her mother – Evelyn's grandmother – had no real understanding of the dangers involved or she would not have agreed to the ride. Mother's own mother had died soon after birth, and Pearl knew she had been reared by Pearl's great-grandparents. Pearl knew they had always been over-protective of her mother, so much so that her mother had never even been allowed to ride a horse.

30. The Rodeo

They rode in the parade and felt very important to be a part of the colorful procession.

The professional rodeo people were resplendent in their outfits. Amateur contestants were riding in great numbers. The Indians were in their best regalia. Cavalrymen from Fort Warren rode their gleaming mounts, lined up in regular ranks, the horses keeping in step.

Pearl was especially thrilled to see the Indians up close. She had seen their many tepees in a field near the rodeo grounds. They added a lot to the spectacle. It was fitting that they should be there in large numbers, she thought. All this country was once theirs. She had read a lot about Plains Indians who had lived in Wyoming and nearby states, following the buffalo which numbered in the millions and getting their food, clothing, blankets, tepees and tools from the meat, skins, and bones of the great beasts. When white settlers moved in and coveted the land, they killed the buffalo and drove out the Indians because they resisted their encroachments. In the 1880's the Indians were put onto reservations where it was impossible for them to live in their traditional ways. She thought this was sad and unjust.

Calf riding was the first event on the program. There were twenty-five events altogether, counting the parade as the first on the program. The girls were listed under the heading, "Calf Riding for Boys under 16." Their names were the first three listed. People must have wondered why anyone named boys Christine, Arlynn and Pearl.

They waited on the track in front of the grandstand. When the time came, some men helped them get on the calves, and put into their hands a rope looped around the calf with a slip knot. They must hold this rope taut and hang onto it. The calves bucked, but the ride was over before they knew it, and they were helped off. They would ride again the next day. It was fun.

One by one the events of the rodeo followed. All of them were interesting. Pearl liked the wild horse race; it was comical. Some of the horses would run the wrong way and some would not run at all. Some bucked and threw their riders who got back on if they could. One horse ran almost to the finish line, then turned and ran back toward the starting point.

As each event took place Pearl was thinking about Evelyn. Would her bull ride go well? She felt sure that everyone was worried, but no one talked about it.

A beautiful part of the rodeo was the exhibition of horsemanship by the cavalry. The horses were fine animals. Their saddles and bridles were oiled and polished 'til they shone. The uniformed riders rode beautifully. They performed precision drill routines that were unbelievably complex. Pearl liked this especially well, because the animals were not hurt or frightened, and the riders were not risking any injuries.

The bucking horse event was scary. The horses went mad; this was because they had flank straps tied around them. These straps hurt them. The same bucking horses were used in many rodeos throughout the country and probably would not buck if they were not suffering. Pearl noticed that when a ride was over, a man on horseback would dash up and loosen the strap. Then the horse would just stand there or calmly walk away.

The bucking rules called for constant raking of the

sides of the horse with spurs, and the rider must hold his hat in his free hand and swing it back and forth in a wide arc. This was called "fanning" the horse. The riders whooped it up too. The horses sunfished: that is, they put their heads down and twisted first to one side and then to the other side in rapid succession, bucking always. It was no wonder that the horses went mad with the strap, the spurs, the hat waving and the noise. It was hard to believe that some of the contestants could actually stay on during this jarring ride. Most of the riders had had many bones broken and had received many other serious injuries.

The bulldogging was very dangerous. One horseman had the job of hazing the animal, keeping it on a more or less straight run. The other rider must come alongside the running animal, leap off his horse, grab the animal's horns, and then twist its head until it fell to the ground.

It was finally time for event number nine, the riding of the Brahma bulls. When Evelyn was in the chute the announcer on the loudspeaker was dramatic in announcing her ride. Pearl held her breath. The bull shot out of the chute and bucked vigorously. Evelyn stayed on, holding tightly to the rope around its belly. Why didn't the pick-up man rescue her? It seemed to Pearl that the ride was long. It probably was only a few seconds. One of the pick-up men made a swift dash and effortlessly lifted her up in front of him. The crowd applauded wildly. Pearl clapped hardest of all. They were all proud of her and glad it was over.

The names of the contestants in this event were not listed on the program. However, one newspaper gave "Fair Evelyn's" ride special mention the next day.

The many events of the rodeo took a long time. But they were varied and interesting. Three of the events were exclusively for Indians. Event number six was the "Indian Buck Race." Number eleven was the "Indian Squaw Race," and event number fifteen was the "Indian Relay Race." The contestants were all Sioux Indians from the Rosebud Reservation in South Dakota. Their names were wonderful. Pearl especially liked these: Dan Charging Bear, Charles Brave Hawk, Oscar Spirited Eagle, Fanny Four Feathers, Troublesome Hawk, and Winnie Little Thunder.

There were some familiar names on the program. King Merritt was a contestant in the step roping contest and Don Brownell, a neighbor of Marie's, rode in the wild horse race.

The trick riding was exciting. The riders seemed to be able to do anything on their horses. That year western movie star Ken Maynard gave an exhibition of trick and fancy riding. He was dressed in a showy black and white outfit and the trappings of his horse gleamed with sliver.

It was good to go to the Dunns' and rest when the rodeo was over. That night the Dunns drove the girls to the city hall to get their pay. The courthouse was brightly lighted. The contestants were gathering on the lawn. The girls felt grown up and important as they got in line and picked up their pay – $1.00 for calf riding. Evelyn got more, of course, but not very much. Big money went to winners of timed, competitive events. There were entry fees for these. There were world champions at Cheyenne.

The day after the rodeo was over the Dunns drove Mother and Arlynn out to the homestead and stayed for a visit with Marie. Evelyn and Pearl rode home.

31. Farewell

Summer was almost over. Pearl's mother had gone home and everyone missed her loving and pleasant ways. Pearl almost decided to go home with her but remembered she had the responsibility of helping Evelyn with the ponies. The girls had ridden all of them, but they wanted to gentle as many as possible so they would get the extra ten dollars that Mr. Farthing had promised. When the time came that Pearl must leave, they would ride to the Farthing ranch and get their pay. Then Mr. Farthing would come after the ponies.

Edna was still in Wyoming. Some of the time she was at the homestead, but she took some trips into the mountains with friends. She decided to stay around until the end of the summer so Pearl could ride home with her. Pearl thought the trip home in the old Tin Lizzy would be lots of fun. Neither of them had ever taken a long auto trip. The fact that they would be crossing Nebraska in the searing heat of August, in a car with no top, did not worry her at all.

When an offer was made to Marie to cook at a big ranch, she asked Edna if she would be willing to stay at the homestead while she was gone. She needed money to buy hay and feed for the livestock during the winter. When Edna agreed to stay with Jackie and the girls, Marie left.

A week after Marie had left, they were surprised that she came back in a car one evening to see how everything was going. The man who brought her was Les Thomsen who was working at the same ranch. He was a little younger than Marie. He had dark curly hair and grey-blue eyes. His teeth were very white and perfect although he had never been to a dentist. Les became a frequent visitor, bringing Marie to the homestead every few days. Everyone enjoyed these visits. Les was lively and full of fun. They especially enjoyed his tales of adventure. He had left home when quite young. His people were of Danish ancestry and lived in the country in Minnesota, where bears and wolves still roamed the woods. He was an outdoorsman and an excellent hunter. When Marie wanted rabbits he could kill them with one shot through the head.

He had lived in many parts of the U.S., earning his living at various jobs. The previous winter he had worked for the U.S. government, feeding hay to the large herd of elk in Jackson Hole country. He had panned for gold in Idaho.

He always found work wherever he was. If there was a job opening and he had not had experience in doing the kind of work offered, he accepted the job and found out how to do it. Then he tackled it with confidence. He was a hard-working man. He pitched in and helped with everything at the homestead.

Everyone soon realized that Les and Marie were in love. Marie was greatly changed. She seemed years younger and was happy all the time. No one was surprised to hear that they were planning to marry.

Pearl and Edna discussed this new development. They wondered if Les would be content to stay on the homestead when he was used to traveling freely all over the country. Pearl was anxious about the prospect of Marie's leaving the homestead because she loved it so much. Edna thought it would be a good thing; there was no real future there. Homesteaders could not make money; they could barely make a living by working hard.

Edna made Pearl realize that Marie would be alone on the homestead when her children were grown. Marie was in her early thirties and should not go through life alone. Edna reminded Pearl that she should think of her own future. She should study hard and do a lot of reading to prepare for college.

Thoughts of the future appealed to Pearl in some ways, but in other ways it all seemed too serious. The responsibilities of the future contrasted with the adventures and fun she enjoyed on the homestead. She did not altogether look forward to the loss of carefree youth.

She told Edna, "I do feel more grown-up now. Evelyn and I have been running a business this summer breaking ponies, and we worked on a haying crew at a ranch. We sold milk too. These were my first real jobs, other than babysitting. I think I've learned a lot about taking responsibility and sticking to a difficult task until it's done. While we were training the ponies, they were teaching us patience and persistence."

"Pearl," Edna said. "You've said you'd like to live in Wyoming. Summers are fine here. Winters must be grim though. You can't live an outdoor life then. You love to read, Pearl. In the city you have the library with an unlimited number of wonderful books. Also you have many friends. You go to plays and movies. And there's music; you love music. You'd miss all that if you lived here."

Pearl began thinking seriously of the future. She wanted a good education and a good job. Her five older sisters and her brothers seemed so independent. She thought they could do anything they wanted to do. She envied them and wanted to be independent too.

Finally there was only one day left before Edna and she must leave. Pearl asked Evelyn to ride all over the homestead with her. They rode Tiny and Waltina and went to the buffalo wallow, to the watering hole, the spring, the garden and all up and down the draw. Then they went up into the breaks to see the Indian campground and the cave with the little spring. Frequently they stopped to walk a while. They saw the cattle and horses and ponies grazing in different groups.

Pearl rejoiced in the feel of the strong Wyoming wind, the intense sunshine, the smell of the sagebrush. She knew she was saying farewell to all these things. Evelyn and she had enjoyed freedom, adventures, and experiences that few teenage girls had ever experienced. They had formed a special bond through working and playing together. Never would they forget these magical summers.

That evening after the chores were done and the family had gathered together in the house, she stepped outside to watch her last glorious Wyoming sunset. The immense sky changed from brilliant color to color – red, orange, purple, yellow, pink – as the sun sank ever lower. Elation and sadness mingled in her heart.

The next morning her eyes filled with tears as she said goodbye to Marie, Evelyn, Arlynn and Jackie. She wondered when and where she would see them again. A chapter of her life had closed, but new experiences awaited her.

The End

Afterword

This book is based on my several summers at my sister Marie's homestead in Wyoming. I have told of incidents that took place during these summers as though they all occurred in one summer.

When I wrote the first copy of this book I wrote it as a book for children. Later I decided to make it more of a family story and also include some of Phebe's, Edna's, Ruth's, and Elisabeth's (Betty's) experiences in Wyoming. All relatives who read the book will find something not entirely accurate.

Obviously, I made up all the conversation since I could not remember exactly what was said, but the occurrences narrated really happened. Some changes that I made are:

> The pony Blackie was actually called Nigger. In my youth the word had no more meaning to me than the name I replaced it with.

> Arlynn moved from Iowa to Wyoming to live with her mother when she was about 13. On an earlier trip, however, she did ride back from Wyoming with Edna and me in the Model T, to attend McKinley Junior High School one more year.

> The still that Evelyn showed me was actually on the homestead, and it was Jack's still. He probably made some money selling bootleg whiskey or maybe he just used it for himself and friends.

Evelyn and I did not arrive at Altus just after the little girl was bitten by the rattlesnake. We learned of it later.

Phebe, Edna, and Betty all wrote letters at my request describing their experiences in Wyoming. As additional sources, I had letters that Ruth, Marie, and Betty had written to Mother from Wyoming. Arlynn supplied me with some facts that I requested.

The initial impetus for my writing came from my grandson, Mark Barrett, who wanted me to write the story of my life. I began with this and maybe will cover my whole life, for him, strictly in journal form.

I regret that Marie, Ruth and Evelyn are not alive to read the book. They were very much alive in my memory as I wrote it.

Pearl Mirich
1994

About the Author

Pearl Rumble was born December 8th, 1910, in Mount Vernon, Iowa, the youngest of the eight children of Pearl Dodge Rumble and Clarence H. Rumble. The family moved to Cedar Rapids in 1917. She graduated from Cornell College in 1933, Phi Beta Kappa, B.A., and taught high school in Illinois from 1935 to 1940.

Pearl married Mark Mirich on June 19, 1937, in Golden, Colorado, and they had two daughters. When her husband died in 1948 she returned to teaching language arts and social studies in Cedar Rapids. She attended summer sessions at the University of Iowa, earning an M.A. in English in 1955. After her retirement she taught English as a second language from 1980 to 1985.

Pearl was a member of the Unitarian Church and active in a number of organizations, including the American Federation of Teachers, NOW, The Women's Political Caucus, League of Women Voters, NAACP, ACLU, the Democratic Party, Common Cause and Public Citizen.

Pearl traveled extensively throughout her life, including trips across the U.S. and Europe. When relations with China thawed in the 1970's she was one of the first American citizens to visit that country.

On November 26, 2009, fifty weeks into her 99th year, Pearl Mirich passed away at home in Iowa City, Iowa.

www.ingramcontent.com/pod-product-compliance
Lightning Source LLC
Chambersburg PA
CBHW030552080526
44585CB00012B/353